UNDERSTANDING MAPS

Charting the Land, Sea, and Sky

UNDERSTANDING

CHARTING THE LAND, SEA,

by Beulah Tannenbaum

New York Toronto London · Whittlesey House

MAPS

AND SKY

and Myra Stillman

Illustrated by Rus Anderson

McGraw-Hill Book Company, Inc.

UNDERSTANDING MAPS:
CHARTING THE LAND, SEA, AND SKY

Library of Congress Catalog Card Number: 57-8632

Published by Whittlesey House
A division of the McGraw-Hill Book Company, Inc.
Printed in the United States of America

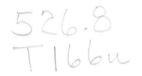
Contents

1. The Why and How of Maps

Across the face of the earth there is an ever-moving stream of traffic. Every second of every day planes, cars, trains, and ships rush over the land and sea. No one can even guess how many people are traveling at this very minute. Perhaps you have seen pictures of night traffic along a busy highway. Each car leaves its own trail of light across the film.

If you had a film on which each man who had ever traveled left such a trail of light, the whole earth would look like a bowl of hopelessly tangled spaghetti. Prehistoric man on foot, a Pacific Islander in an outrigger canoe, the pilot of a jet plane, your father in his car, each would have left his bright trail.

Whether a man jogs along on foot, glides on metal wings, or steers an ocean liner, there are certain basic things which he must know. Through the ages, man has found three things which help him reach his destination: *direction, distance,* and *landmarks.* He has learned to use all three in a picture which is called a *map.*

Maps are so much a part of daily life that people seldom stop to think about them. But just imagine a world without maps! Suppose you had to describe the shape of your state without drawing a map. Unless you live in Colorado or Wyoming, you would find it very difficult. Or, just think of planning a trip from Atlanta, Georgia, to Seattle, Washington, without a map.

No one knows when the first map was drawn, but certainly it was long before there was any written history. When primitive man wanted to tell the rest of his tribe how to find a special hunting ground, he needed to show distance, direction, and landmarks. To do this, he drew a map in the dirt with a stick. In Biblical times, the sailors made their own maps to help them find their way around the Mediterranean Sea. By the time Columbus was ready to sail from Spain, he could get expensive hand-drawn maps from the few map makers of Europe. Today's ocean liner needs a special chartroom for its many maps. But whether maps are traced in the dirt, hand-drawn on parchment, or printed on paper, they all have three things in common. They guide the traveler by picturing clearly direction, distance, and landmarks.

If you want to plan a trip by car, you can go to any gas station and get a free road map that will give you the three basic facts needed by travelers. Part of the map might look like the one on the next page.

To plan a trip from New City to Northport, the first thing you need to know is in which direction to travel. Road maps usually place north at the top, but to be sure, look on the map for the *compass rose* which

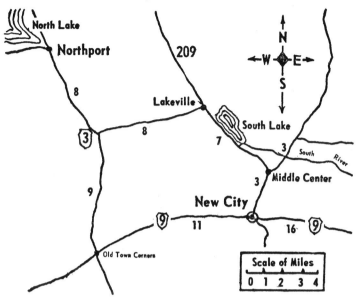

points to the north. You can see that Northport is northwest of New City.

Next, you need to know how far you will have to travel. You can find the distance by adding the miles which are printed in small unboxed numbers alongside of the road lines. These numbers tell the mileage between such landmarks as cities and crossroads. For example, it is 3 miles from New City to Middle Center and 11 miles from New City to Old Town Corners.

There is no direct road from New City to Northport, but there are two possible routes. If you go in a northerly direction, the first landmark you will reach is Middle Center. Turn left and travel 7 miles past

South Lake to Lakeville. Turn left again and continue for 8 miles to Route 3. Turn right and follow Route 3 north 8 miles more to Northport. You could also reach Northport by traveling west from New City for 11 miles on Route 9. Then, turn right at Old Town Corners and follow Route 3 north for 17 miles to Northport.

The map can help you decide which road to take. If you start out in a northerly direction, the distance is 26 miles. The scenery probably will be interesting because you will drive along the shore of South Lake, but you will have to go through two villages. The road from Lakeville to Route 3 is not a state road for it has no route number. It probably will not be as good a road as those which are numbered. If you choose the other route, the distance is 28 miles, and you will go through only one village. There are no landmarks like South Lake to give you a clue to the scenery, but you know that you will travel on good roads, for both of them are numbered state highways.

It is simple enough with this road map to plan your trip from New City to Northport. With road maps you can get free from your local gas station, or from their main office, it would not be difficult for you to plan a trip across the United States. This was not always true. As recently as forty years ago, it would have been impossible.

In the early days of automobiles, all you could do

was start out in the right general direction and stop at each crossroad to ask your way. Some of the crossroads had markers, many of which were faded by rain and sun and could hardly be read. Sometimes a traveler caught at night on a dark road had to climb a pole and light a match to read a weather-beaten sign. One traveler tells of shinnying up a pole on a wet and stormy night only to find he had left his matches in the car. On the second attempt and three matches later, he finally read the sign. It was an ad for chewing tobacco.

It is easy enough to plan a trip with the information you can read from a road map. But how does the map maker collect this information? How does he measure distance and determine direction? To understand the problems of the map maker, try to imagine what you would do if you were dropped by rocket ship on a strange planet with instructions to map its surface. The earth was just such an unknown vast expanse to early man. This book is the story of how and why man learned to map his strange planet, Earth.

2. Distance, Direction, and Landmarks

You can read distance from a map because you and the map maker agree on a unit of measure. An *inch* means a definite distance to both of you. Because you use a ruler so often, you know there are 12 inches in a *foot* without having to figure it out each time. You also know that there are 3 feet in a *yard*. And even though you probably have never measured a mile yourself, you have learned that there are 5,280 feet in a *mile*. Today the unit of measure which we call a "foot" covers the same distance whether it is used in England, Florida, or Alaska. This was not always true. One hundred fifty years ago in Europe, the foot measure came in 280 different sizes.

The story of how man worked out fixed measurements covers thousands of years. The earliest units were based on parts of the human body. The length of the forearm, the marching pace of a soldier, and even the size of a king's foot were used as units of measurement. You can imagine the confusion which occurred when the old king died and the new king's foot became the standard.

It was not until 1824, when the English Parliament set up a new standard, that the present length of the yard was finally accepted. The modern standard ruler is kept in London. It is made of brass and has a gold button at each end. The distance between the buttons is exactly one yard.

While the English were deciding the exact length of the yard, the people of France were working out another way of measuring distance. They wanted their measures to depend on something which would never change. Instead of using a part of the human body, they decided to use the earth itself. The French system is based on the *meter*. A meter is one ten-millionth of the length of a line starting at the North Pole, running through Paris, and ending at the equator. A meter is just a little longer than a yard. It is 39.37 inches.

In a safe in Paris there is a platinum bar exactly one meter long. This is the official standard for the meter. Even though the meter is not commonly used in America, there is an exact copy of it in the U.S. Bureau of Standards in Washington, D.C. The official length of the American "yard" is based on this meter stick. Even if both of these meter sticks were destroyed or stolen, it would be easy to make others just exactly the same length.

It took thousands of years of experimenting for man to arrive at fixed standards of measurement. But with this knowledge the map maker can show distance on the map so that anyone can read it. Distance on a road map can be shown in two ways. You may add the small unboxed numbers as you did in finding the distance from New City to Northport, or you may figure the distance by using the *scale* which is found on all maps. The scale tells you how many miles there are in each inch on the map.

Finding the scale is one of the first things a map maker does. He must decide the size of the finished map and he must know the size of the area he is mapping. To find the scale, he divides the size of the area by the size of the map. The answer is the number of miles to the inch or the scale. For example, if you are making a map 100 inches wide of an area which is 1,200 miles wide, the scale would be 1,200 miles divided by 100 inches, or 12 miles to 1 inch.

If you look at the next picture, you will see that, while the maps are the same size, the scales are very different. Because the United States is so much larger, the scale of its map is 480 miles to 1 inch, while that of Connecticut is only 23 miles to 1 inch.

But knowing distance is not enough; the traveler also has to know direction. The captain of a ship has a special problem. There are no familiar hills or buildings to guide him. He has only a trackless waste, and yet a ship can leave Land's End, England, and always sail directly into New York Harbor. This is done with the help of sea maps which are called *charts*.

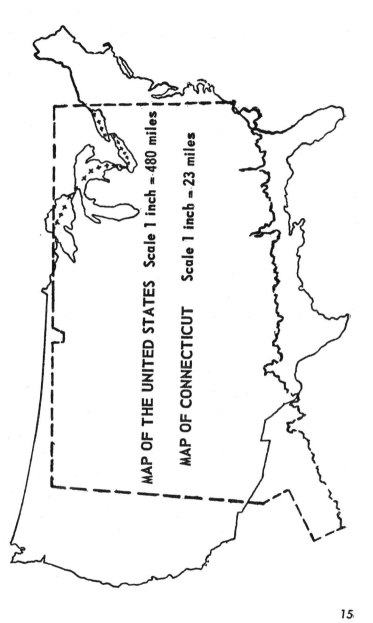

MAP OF THE UNITED STATES   Scale 1 inch = 480 miles

MAP OF CONNECTICUT   Scale 1 inch = 23 miles

Many kinds of sea charts will be explained in Chapter Six.

Today's ships need many complicated instruments as well as charts to help them steer a true course. The sailor who is in charge of plotting the course is called the *navigator* (nav′ee·gay·tor). A navigator spends many years studying before he can be trusted to guide the ship. And yet birds, without maps or instruments, can find their way easily over vast sea and land distances. Birds have an amazing sense of direction. Some North American swallows fly all the way to Argentina each winter, and the next spring are often found again in their old nests.

Man has no such ability, and yet direction is as important to a man who wishes to travel as it is to birds. Earliest man used the rising sun to tell direction. We say that the sun rises in the east, but this is not exactly true. As the earth moves around the sun, the position in which the sun rises changes slightly each day. In the Northern Hemisphere, during the summer the sun rises north of east, and in the winter, south of east. But no matter where the sun rises, one thing is always true. If a stick is put into the ground so that it stands straight up, it will cast its shortest shadow at noon. This noonday shadow will point due north every day of the year.

This way of finding direction was helpful on land, but it did not solve the problem for the sailor. You

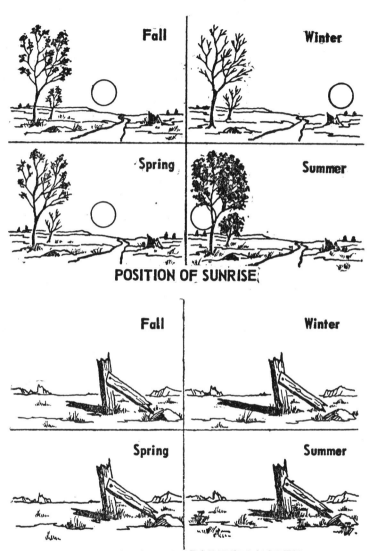

Fall

Winter

Spring

Summer

POSITION OF SUNRISE

Fall

Winter

Spring

Summer

NOON DAY SHADOW POINTING NORTH

can imagine what would happen if a sailor on a little ship tossing on a rough sea tried to find north in this way. If man wished to travel on the water, he needed a better guide.

While watching the heavens, the men of ancient times discovered a strange fact. As the stars wheel around in the night sky, one star always seems to stay in the same place. No matter where you stand in the Northern Hemisphere, whether it is outside your house, or at the other end of town, or in Paris, or Vladivostok, or Alaska, this star is always in the north. It is called the *North* or *Pole Star*.

NOW TRY THIS

You can find the Pole Star very easily. On a clear night, look toward the north for the Big Dipper. It is made of seven stars. The two stars in the cup which are farthest from the handle are called the pointers. If you could draw a line through these stars, it would lead to the last star in the handle of the Little Dipper. This star, which is not as bright as the pointers, is the North Star.

When the sky was cloudy, neither the sun nor the stars could help the sailor. Then the winds were used to tell direction. Old maps often have pictures of the four main winds of the Mediterranean area. These show direction on a map in much the same way as our

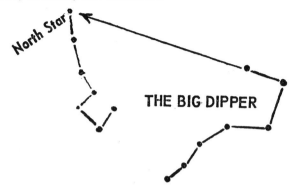

FINDING THE POLE STAR

present compass signs. But these winds all felt, smelled, and sounded the same. Since they could not talk and tell their names, a sailor far at sea could not always be sure which wind was blowing. What man needed was something he could use night or day, rain or shine, on land or on sea.

The answer to this problem was the *compass*. No one knows who invented the compass. The honor has been claimed by many nations, and it is probable that there were many different inventors. We do know that in the Ural Mountains of eastern Europe, a very strange kind of stone is found. Many people thought it was a magic stone for two reasons. First, it can pull iron toward itself. Second, if a long thin piece is mounted so that it can move freely, it will always point toward the north. It was given the name *lodestone* (load'-

EURUS
The East Wind

BOREAS
The North Wind

NOTUS
The South Wind

ZEPHYRUS
The West Wind

stone), or lead stone, because it could lead travelers by pointing direction. Today it is called *magnetite* (mag'nuh·tight). A little magnetite is found with other iron ores in many places on earth. There is a large deposit of magnetite in Magnetic Cove, Arkansas.

No one knows exactly what magnetism is, but for more than 300 years scientists have been studying magnets and have discovered many facts about them. They have found that the magnetism is strongest at the ends, or *poles,* of a magnet, and that if you break a magnet in half, each part will be a magnet with two poles. If you break the two new magnets in half again, you will have four magnets, and so on down to the smallest piece you can get.

When scientists are not certain of an explanation, they call it a *theory.* They use a theory as long as it explains all the known facts. Many scientists accept the theory that the *molecules* (mol'uh·kules), the groups of atoms, of which magnetite is made are all facing in one direction. This gives a magnet two unlike ends: a "north" end and a "south" end. If you place two pieces of magnetite close to each other with opposite poles facing, they will attract each other. If like ends are placed close together, they will repel each other.

Even though no one knows the exact reason, the earth also acts like a huge magnet with one pole on Prince of Wales Island in northern Canada and the other in Wilkes Land in Antarctica. And so a compass needle will always point north because its "north-

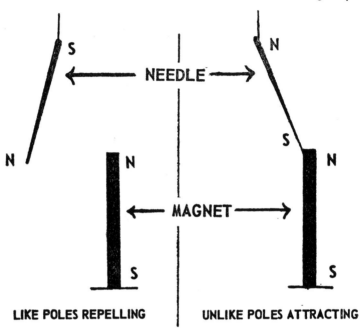

| LIKE POLES REPELLING | UNLIKE POLES ATTRACTING |

seeking" end is attracted to the earth's north magnetic pole.

The earliest compasses were made by fastening a sliver of lodestone shaped like a needle to a reed. This was then floated in a bowl of water. During the Middle Ages, trade between Europe and the Orient became important. The kings and knights wanted rich silks to wear and spices for their foods. The trade routes across the great deserts of Asia were traveled by camel caravans. Leading most of these caravans were the owners of such compasses. They kept their lodestones a carefully hidden secret so that they were looked upon as great magicians. It was so difficult to cross the great deserts without this "magic" that the guides were able to charge very high prices for their services.

These compasses were very clumsy. On a rough sea the water splashing in the bowl made them very hard to use. The next step was to find an easier way to float the lodestone. A round base was made on which directions were marked. In the center was a raised point called a pivot. A small dent was made in the center of the lodestone and this was balanced on the pivot. The stone could now move freely and point to north without the use of water. The compasses you can buy now are made in much the same way, but a needle of magnetized steel is used instead of a lodestone.

NOW TRY THIS

You can make your own compass by stroking a darning needle with a magnet. You must be sure to stroke the needle in only one direction for about three minutes. Always use the same end of the magnet for each stroke. In this way, you will make the molecules of the needle line up in one direction. When the needle will attract a paper clip, it is ready. Run the needle through a small piece of cork and then float it in a bowl of water. One end of the needle will always point north.

Today a picture of a compass is placed on a map to help you find direction. This is called a *compass rose*. Suppose you are stranded in the middle of a strange crossroad and you do not know which of the four roads will take you home. If you have a map and a compass, it will be easy to find your way. First find north with your compass. Then hold the map so that the arrow on the compass rose points north. Now you can see which of the four roads will lead you home. When you use a map and compass this way, you are *orienting* the map.

If you do not have a compass, you may use landmarks to help you find direction. A *landmark* can be anything that is used as a guide. For example, if you came out of the woods on the road between Middle Center and Lakeville and did not know which way to go, you could use the map on page 9 to help you. If South Lake is on your right as you follow the road, you know that you must be heading northwest. If it is on your left, you are traveling southeast.

Since primitive times, landmarks have been used in map making. If man could travel like a bird in a straight line, he would need to know only direction and distance. But imagine what might happen if you wanted to tell a friend how to find his way to your home. If you told him to go straight east for one-half mile, he might find himself jumping over fences, climbing roof tops, and even swimming a pond. On land, direction and distance are not enough; landmarks are needed.

Landmarks were important also in the history of sea travel. Before the invention of the compass, sailors tried to stay within sight of land. They learned to know each high cliff and church steeple. This kind of sailing was called *church steeple navigation* and the guides were called landmarks.

Many old maps have pictures of landmarks on them such as the ones in the illustration. Usually, road maps do not have these pictures, but they do show landmarks. Each city marked on the map, each lake, river, or railroad crossing is a landmark for to-day's traveler. Some modern maps use certain symbols to show landmarks such as those on the next page.

Indicating Mission or Church

Indicating Colony Settlement

Indicating Mountains

16th CENTURY

LANDMARKS USED ON OLD MAPS

✈   **Airports**

•   **Points of Interests**

🏛   **State Parks**

🛡   **U. S. Interstate Highways**

🌲   **State Forests**

▲   **Colleges and Universities**

20th CENTURY
LANDMARKS ON MODERN MAPS

You probably have many of your own special landmarks that help you find places. Perhaps you always
turn left at "that yellow gas station" when you visit
your grandparents. Or, you may always turn right at
the "candy store" on your way to the library. In this
case, the "yellow gas station" and the "candy store"
are your landmarks.

The trouble with landmarks is that they do not last
forever. A house or a store may burn down; small
railroads sometimes stop running and their tracks are
ripped up for scrap metal; trees die and rot away.
Even a stream may dry up or change its course. While
landmarks are an important part of map making, they
are less dependable than direction and distance.

Disappearing landmarks often cause trouble to

land owners and the *surveyors* who measure the land. Most old deeds use landmarks to describe property. Such a deed may read "... bounded northerly by a line beginning at the mouth of Lewis Creek or Kill and running thence south 85 degrees east to a large oak tree." After 150 years, the oak tree and its stump have disappeared and the mouth of the creek may have moved many yards.

Because natural landmarks change easily, the U.S. Coast and Geodetic (gee'oh·det'ik) Survey which makes official maps of the United States has its own landmarks. These are called *bench marks*. A bench mark is usually a bronze plaque set in rock or concrete. It is shown on a geodetic survey map by an X followed by the initials B.M.

Fixed standards of measurement, methods of determining direction, and an understanding of the use of landmarks are the tools which the modern map maker has inherited from the past. With this information, you could map the land on which your house is

BENCH MARK

BENCH MARK IN A ROCK ALONG A ROAD

built. By measuring the distance between landmarks with a tape measure and finding the direction with a compass, you could make an accurate map. The map maker, however, cannot walk from landmark to landmark with a tape measuring continents and oceans, but he has found ways to map them.

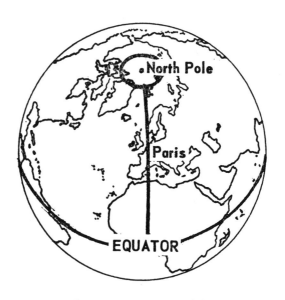

THE PARIS MERIDIAN

The meter is one ten-millionth of this line from the North Pole to the equator.

3. Mapping the Land

Although it takes many years for most natural landmarks to change or disappear, there are places in the
world where landmarks may change overnight. The
men who climbed Mt. Everest in May, 1953, marked
their trails with colored flags driven deeply into the
ice. During the night, the great glacier would shift
and crack as the ice flowed down the mountain. The
next morning the men might find some of their flags
still standing in the ice, but at the bottom of new
crevasses 200 or 300 feet below. And so, the work
had to be done all over again and new landmarks set
up.

There are many other strange things about this,
the highest mountain in the world. If you look at the
latest maps, you will find that Mt. Everest is 29,141
feet high. Older maps list the mountain as 29,002
feet. What happened to increase the size of the giant
since it was first surveyed in 1852? There are two
possible answers.

Perhaps Mt. Everest is growing! We often think
that mountains are so great and strong that nothing
can change them, but this is just not true. Like other
landmarks, mountains change. Some are worn away
by weather and become smaller. The Himalaya

(him·ah·lay'ah) Range, of which Mt. Everest is a part, is still young. These mountains are still being pushed up from the earth. Mt. Everest may have grown 139 feet in the last hundred years.

It is also possible that the first surveyors were wrong. Certainly, they had to work under the most difficult conditions. Their instruments were not as good as those which are used today. They had no airplanes to help them, and they could not enter the two countries at the base of Mt. Everest. Tibet, on the north, was closed to travelers until 1920, and Nepal, on the south, would not permit anyone to enter until after the Second World War. In spite of these problems, they were able to estimate very closely the height of the mountain.

The men who survey the land for map making are called *geodetic surveyors*. Their work is most exciting and adventurous. Maybe we do not read about them in the newspapers as often as we read about famous mountain-climbing expeditions and jungle safaris, but often the surveyor has explored the area before the "adventurer" arrives. This was true recently in Central America, where a party of climbers announced with great fanfare in the local papers that they were planning to be the first to climb a high mountain in that province. The climb was successful, but it was never reported in the newspapers, for, when they reached the peak, they found the bronze bench mark of the Inter-American Geodetic Survey set in the bed rock. The surveyors had been there before them!

Perhaps you think all of the world has been mapped and there is nothing left for the surveyors to do. Such an idea is very wrong indeed. As a matter of fact, you may live in a part of the United States which has not yet been mapped by the U.S. Geological Survey. Although we have some kind of map for every part of the United States, many of them were first made a long time ago. But landmarks have changed and instruments are much better today. As a result, experts believe that only about 37 per cent of the United States is mapped accurately.

If there is much work ahead in the United States, there is even more in the rest of the world. Some areas of Asia, Africa, and South America have never been mapped. In 1891, a plan for a universal map was discussed at a meeting in Berne, Switzerland. By 1913, it was agreed that the nations of the world would work together on such a map. It was to be made up of 1,500 sheets or separate maps, all using a scale of 1,000,000:1, or 1 kilometer on land would be shown as 1 millimeter on the map. At present, only about 400 sheets have been finished. As you can see, there is still plenty of work for the map makers. If you want to help with this work when you are older, there will be many unsurveyed lands waiting for you.

There are many problems in measuring the land and so man has had to invent many ways of doing it. One method is actually to measure the ground with some kind of ruler. For example, the Egyptians had an unusual problem. Each year the Nile River flooded its banks and washed away the landmarks which divided the fields. After the flood had passed, it was necessary to remeasure all this rich valley land. In order to make the job easier, and be sure everyone had his fair share and paid the right taxes, the Egyptians used ropes of exactly the same length to measure the fields each year. Today, in the pyramids, which are the tombs of the ancient Egyptian kings, you can see pictures of the men at work measuring the land.

When George Washington was employed to survey the American wilderness, a standard surveyor's chain 66 feet long was used. Today, a steel tape 100 or 200 feet in length has replaced the chain. This tape method is accurate for measuring short level distances, but most of the distances which the geodetic surveyors must measure are neither short nor level.

NOW TRY THIS

To see for yourself how much difference levelness makes, try an "ant's-eye view" of a landscape. Put two sticks into the ground and make "ant" mountains by placing stones or boxes between them. Measure the distance between the sticks with a tape measure. (If you do not have a tape, a piece of string will do.) Be sure that the tape goes up and down over the tops and sides of the boxes or stones. Now remove the "mountains" and measure the distance between the sticks again. You may be surprised to discover how great the difference is.

It was easy enough for you to move the stones or boxes, but the geodetic surveyors cannot move mountains and valleys. They need more than a tape measure to find the distance between two places on the earth's surface.

The shape of the earth also causes trouble for the surveyors. Because it is round, a traveler who wishes to go in a straight line from New York to Chicago would have to tunnel through the earth. Since he cannot do this easily, he has to travel on the surface and he needs to know the distance along a line which follows the earth's curve.

Since the earth is so large, the amount of curve at any one place is slight, and in measuring very short distances, surveyors can act as if the earth were flat. In measuring greater distances, the curve of the earth becomes very important. In the diagram you can see what happens when there is a big curve between two points. The distance between *A* and *B* on the straight line is 3 inches. On the curved line it is 3½ inches.

In order to solve these problems of land measure-

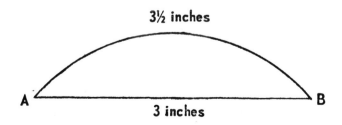

3½ inches

A   B

3 inches

ment, the geodetic surveyors use a special way of measuring called *triangulation* (try·ang'you·lay'shun). This name comes from the word triangle. A *triangle* is a figure with three straight sides. The corners are called *angles*.

Several thousand years ago, mathematicians began to study triangles. They discovered many interesting things about them. For example, they found that if they knew the length of one side of a triangle and the sizes of two of the angles, they could figure out the lengths of the other two sides without measuring them. Modern geodetic surveyors use this fact when they want to find the straight distance between two points on land in spite of hills, valleys, and the curvature of the earth.

In triangulation, three surveyors work together. One is at each corner of the triangle. The distance between two of the surveyors is measured very carefully with a steel tape. It is called the *base line*. A level area such as a straight road is usually chosen for the base line. U.S. Geodetic Surveyors measure the base line thirty-two times to be sure their measurement is correct.

Each surveyor, standing at his corner of the triangle, has a *theodolite* (the·ah'do·lite). This contains a telescope and an angle-measuring instrument, and because levelness is so important, it also has a very good leveling device. The men measure the angles by using their theodolites. When they know the length of one side and the sizes of two of the angles, it is easy for them to work out the lengths of the other two sides. Using either of these sides as the new base, the surveyors make a new triangle and continue across the country.

Triangulation is often done at night. Each surveyor has a powerful light so that the others can see

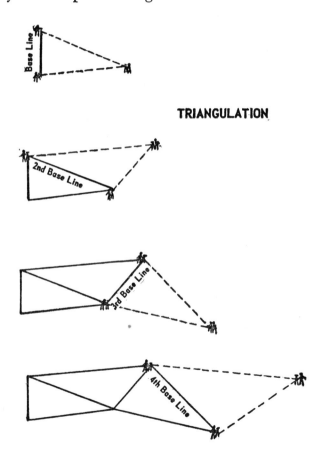

TRIANGULATION

him easily through their theodolites, and be able to measure their angles. Lights on mountain tops can be seen for a greater distance than lights on flat land. For this reason, a triangle usually measures about 10 miles on flat land and about 50 miles in the mountains.

Triangulation is also used to find *altitude* (which means height) as well as the size of the land. The surveyor does the actual measuring as he tramps over mountains and through jungles, but usually other men do the arithmetic and plot the map in an office far away. Sometimes a surveyor does not even know what he has discovered. For example, people had known that the Himalayan mountain, which the natives called *Chomolungma* (cho'mo·lung'mah), and which the chart listed simply as Peak XV, was very high. But it was a clerk in the office of the Indian Trigonometric Survey working with a great pile of figures who suddenly announced that he had discovered the highest mountain in the world. It was named Mt. Everest for Sir George Everest who was in charge of surveying India.

It would be fun if you could measure the height of a mountain by triangulation. Of course, you don't have a Mt. Everest in your back yard, and even if you have a lesser mountain near your home, it would not be easy to do it without a theodolite. However, you can find the height of a tree, a telephone pole, or your house. It would be very difficult to climb up the side and measure it inch by inch, but you can do it by using a form of triangulation. With the help of the table we have worked out, you will be able to find the height of objects which are too tall for you to measure.

NOW TRY THIS

Let's suppose you decide to measure a tree. The materials you will need are a tape measure, a yardstick, two stakes, a very long piece of string, and a friend to work with you. Tie one end of the string to a stake. Measure off 50 feet on the string and then tie it to the other stake. When the string is stretched out straight, the distance between the stakes must be exactly 50 feet. Put one stake in the ground at the foot of the tree. Place the other stake straight out from the

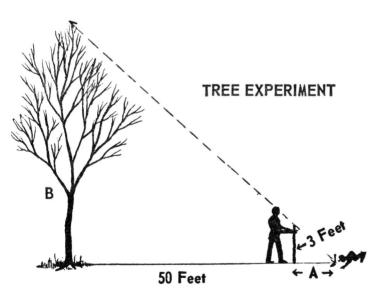

TREE EXPERIMENT

B

←3 Feet

50 Feet

← A →

tree, making sure the string is tight. Kneeling at the second stake and with your eye as close to the ground as possible, sight the top of the tree. Now ask your friend to hold the yardstick straight up and down and move it across the ground along the line of the string.

When the top of the yardstick and the top of the tree are in line, tell him to mark the spot. Then measure the distance from the stake where you were kneeling to the spot he has just marked. In the table, we will call this distance A. Let us suppose the distance A is 29 inches. Look in column A in the table until you find 29 inches. Now find the number on the same line in column B. It is 62 feet. Sixty-two feet is the height of the tree.

This is a rough way of measuring and, although the result may not be accurate, it is close. The slope of the ground and the straightness of the tree and the yardstick are just some of the things which might cause errors. But you do have a fair estimate of the height of the tree. You and your friend are like the surveyors in the field. You have found the measurements. Just as the men in the office do the arithmetic for the surveyors, the table does the arithmetic for you. Also like the surveyors, you have been working with triangles. Look at the picture and you will see that you have used two triangles in measuring.

Mapping mountains is easy compared to the problems the map makers must solve in other parts of our

TABLE FOR FINDING HEIGHTS

A (*Ground distance*)	B (*Height*)
12 inches (1 foot)	150 feet
13 inches	138½ feet
14 inches	128½ feet
15 inches	120 feet
16 inches	112½ feet
17 inches	106 feet
18 inches (1½ feet)	100 feet
19 inches	94¾ feet
20 inches	90 feet
21 inches	85¾ feet
22 inches	81¾ feet
23 inches	78¼ feet
24 inches (2 feet)	75 feet
25 inches	72 feet
26 inches	69¼ feet
27 inches	66⅔ feet
28 inches	64¼ feet
29 inches	62 feet
30 inches (2½ feet)	60 feet
33 inches	54½ feet
36 inches (3 feet)	50 feet
39 inches	46¼ feet
42 inches (3½ feet)	43 feet
45 inches	40 feet
48 inches (4 feet)	37½ feet
4½ feet	33⅓ feet
5 feet	30 feet
5½ feet	27¼ feet
6 feet	25 feet
6½ feet	23 feet
7 feet	21½ feet
7½ feet	20 feet

(The values in column *B* of this table are approximate. They were obtained from the solution of similar triangles.)

globe. For example, maps of the Antarctic show great blank spaces. The surveyors cannot do their jobs easily there because of the large expanse of snow and ice which is constantly shifting and splitting. This was the case when Admiral Byrd returned, in 1955, to the Ross Ice Shelf, which was used as a landing base by his 1947 expedition. He found that a piece of ice 200 miles long and 10 miles wide, about equal in area to the State of Delaware, had cracked off and drifted to sea. And what is more, only the top 10 feet of a 70-foot radio tower built by his men in 1927 could be seen. The rest was buried under the snowfall of thirty years.

Land travel is so difficult in the everlasting ice, snow, and winds of Antarctica that it is not practical to map the continent by triangulation. So the map makers take to the air. Probably map makers have always wished they could fly high above the land they were mapping. The improvement of the camera brought an answer to this dream. Even before the first airplane, surveyors carried cameras as well as theodolites when they scaled such high peaks as the Himalayas and the Canadian Rockies. With these cameras they could take a series of pictures in all directions.

Cameras were also attached to kites and balloons. These photographs were very interesting but not important to map makers since the exact position of the swaying kites and balloons could not be controlled.

They had to wait for the invention of the airplane to obtain really good aerial pictures. The first big photo-flight project began in 1924, when the U.S. Coast and Geodetic Survey used photographs taken from air-planes to map the Mississippi River Delta. The fol-lowing year the Hamilton Rice Expedition was able to map from the air the impassable rain forests around the Rio Negro in Brazil. Whether the pictures are taken on a mountain top or in an airplane, the use of aerial photographs in making maps is called *photo-grammetry* (fo'toe·gram"eh·tree).

A photographic flight must be planned with great care. The area to be mapped is divided into long nar-row sections called *strips.* Each strip is planned so that it will overlap the strip on either side. The pilot must be very skillful, for the plane must fly on a straight line down each strip, and it must be kept ex-actly level at all times.

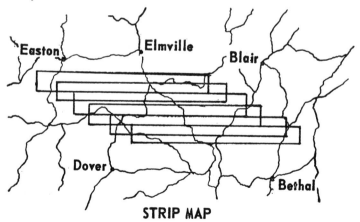

STRIP MAP

Although almost any airplane can be used for this work, a big steady plane that flies slowly is preferred. The camera may be attached to the side, but more often it is placed over a hole in the bottom of the plane. A tremendous roll of film is used. For U.S. Government work, the finished picture is 9 inches square and each roll takes from 100 to 500 pictures.

In planning a flight, the map maker must consider the time of day, the season, the air currents, and the weather. The clearest pictures can be made in the spring or fall, when there are neither leaves on the trees nor snow on the ground. Pictures are taken between 10 A.M. and 2 P.M., when the shadows are shortest. The pilot needs to know all about the air currents above the area. While it might seem that more detailed pictures could be made by flying low, strong currents and air pockets near the ground make it impossible to keep the plane steady and exactly on course. For this reason most flights are made at least 1 mile and often 3 miles above the land. And finally, the weather must be cloudless and clear.

The aerial photographer is like the surveyor; he gathers the information. Then map makers, working in an office often many hundreds of miles away, plot the maps from the photographic strips.

Even with the use of aerial photography, mapping the Antarctic is still a hard problem. Weather conditions are seldom ideal. Sudden snow squalls and gale winds up to 200 miles an hour are not unusual. Antarctica at first glance may seem a useless continent, home only to seals, penguins, and gulls; and yet, men risk their lives, and nations willingly spend millions of dollars to map this trackless wilderness.

This "icebox of the world" is very important in our lives for several reasons. Many major weather conditions start in the polar regions and sweep out across the land and sea. In Chapter Eight, you will learn how the world's weather is made and mapped. Because the North Pole is located in the Arctic Ocean, the permanent weather station farthest north had to be set up on Ellesmere Island, 518 miles from the Pole. The South Pole, however, is located on the continent of Antarctica, so that it is possible to place a station right at the South Pole and record the storms as they are born.

The large, uninhabited continent of Antarctica is also a treasure house of hidden minerals. Airplane surveys have spied iron ore in the mountains beyond the Ross Sea. This section is known as *the area of inaccessibility*. Inaccessible means impossible to reach. But this part of the world was named before the age of modern airplanes, helicopters, and snow tractors. Yesterday's area of inaccessibility can be reached today. Iron ore is probably not the only treasure. Many people believe that valuable metals, oil, nitrates, and even uranium are waiting underneath the snow.

The men who measure the land have to face many problems, but they always have been able to work out an answer. If mountains are in the way, they climb to the top and go on with the triangulation. If the tropical forest is too thick, or the Antarctic snow is too deep, they turn to aerial photography. Each of these methods of land measurement depends in part on landmarks. But only 28 per cent of the earth is land, and the surveyor cannot set up his theodolite on the pitching waves. Even an aerial photograph would not help because a picture of the North Pacific might look exactly the same as one of the South Atlantic. There are no visible landmarks to help, and yet map makers can and do chart the vast expanse of rolling ocean.

4. Mapping the Sea: Finding the Latitude

The ice caps of the polar region, which send blasts of cold weather out over the warmer parts of the earth, also create nightmares for the men who sail the ships. With their wonderful charts, today's sailors can check quickly the coast of the mainland or the location of any island. But far to the north and the south, the polar ice caps feed into the sea temporary islands which are always in motion. These islands of ice, called *icebergs*, are found in many shapes and sizes.

Most of the icebergs which originate in the Antarctic are flat or have slightly rounded tops. They may be as large as the 2,000 square miles which broke from the Ross Ice Shelf or small enough to fit into an ice box. Small icebergs are called *growlers*. But giants or growlers, the icebergs from the Antarctic menace the ships that go around Cape Horn.

The icebergs that break off the glaciers of Greenland look like fairy castles crowned with spires. With only one-ninth of their bulk above the water and a deadly eight-ninths hidden beneath, sprawling in unknown shapes, they sail majestically down the Labrador Current straight into the main shipping lanes that join Europe and America.

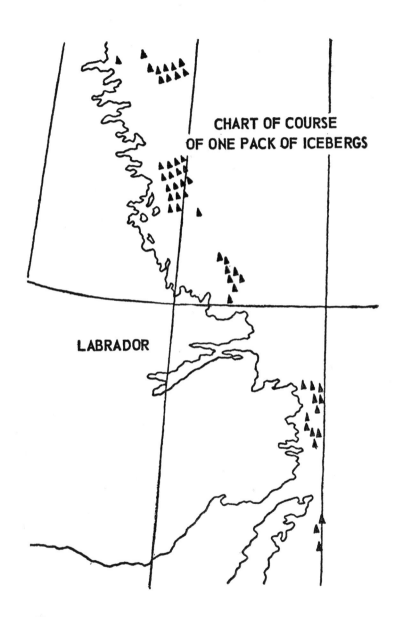

CHART OF COURSE
OF ONE PACK OF ICEBERGS

LABRADOR

46

For many years only the eyes of the lookouts in the crow's-nests, peering into the dreary fog or inky night, protected the ships. Many were wrecked by the silent floating islands. Perhaps the most famous was the *Titanic*, which everyone believed was unsinkable. This great passenger liner, built at a cost of many millions of dollars, sailed from England on April 10, 1912, on her maiden voyage to America. Four days later she was only a wrecked hull lying at the bottom of the North Atlantic, with 1,517 of her 2,224 people lost. An uncharted island of ice had sunk the "unsinkable" ship before she could complete her first voyage.

Lighthouses and maps of the area protect the sailor from the dangers of a rocky shore. Even though icebergs do not come equipped with lighthouses, their positions and probable courses can be mapped. The tragedy of the *Titanic* made people all over the world aware of the danger of icebergs, and as a result, in 1912, the International Ice Patrol was formed. Today its boats and planes prowl the northern seas in search of icebergs. From the information they supply, the U.S. Hydrographic Office issues a monthly "pilot chart" showing the temperature of ocean water and the ice fields located during the previous month. Since these move about so freely, the Hydrographic Office sends out special bulletins to ships at sea whenever necessary.

But the captain of the *Titanic* was not thinking about future maps on that foggy April night. What

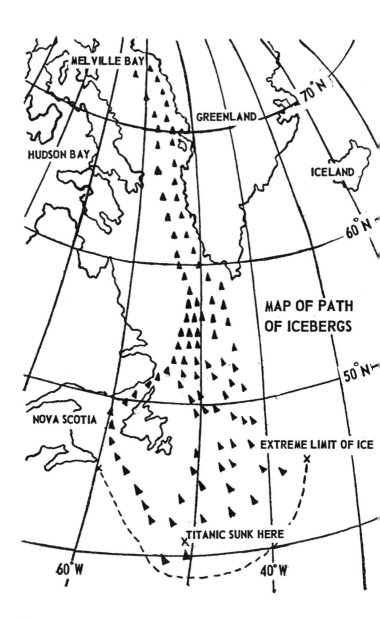

MELVILLE BAY

GREENLAND

70°N

HUDSON BAY

ICELAND

60°N

MAP OF PATH
OF ICEBERGS

50°N

NOVA SCOTIA

EXTREME LIMIT OF ICE

TITANIC SUNK HERE

60°W

40°W

48

he needed was help, and he needed it quickly. If you need help at home, you can call the police or fire department and tell them your street and house number. A ship at sea has no street or house number, or even a city or state name which can identify its location. But each ship has an "address" which changes as the ship moves. And so the wireless on the *Titanic*, sending through the air for the first time in history the new international call for help, "SOS," gave this address: 41°45′ N. Lat.; 50°14′ W. Long. With this information, the steamer *Carpathia* traveled 58 miles across trackless ocean directly to the wrecked *Titanic*.

Suppose you and your friend want to meet on the street so that you can go to the movies together. If he tells you, "Meet me on Main Street," you might find him. But what if Main Street is several miles long! If he says, "Meet me on Maple Avenue," you could have the same problem. But if he tells you to meet him at the corner of Main Street and Maple Avenue, you could find him easily. What you needed to know in order to pin-point your meeting place was two things.

In the same way, if you want to find an exact spot on a piece of paper, two measurements are needed, the distance from the top or bottom of the page and the distance from either side. Suppose you want to start a drawing 1 inch from the top and 1½ inches from the left side. In the diagram on page 50, the line *AB* is 1 inch from the top along its entire length.

The line *CD* is 1½ inches from the left side. No matter how long these lines are drawn, they will meet only at the point *X*.

One inch from the top of the page could be anywhere along the line *AB*. One and one-half inches from the left could be anywhere along the line *CD*. But the point *X* where the lines cross, and only that point, is 1 inch from the top *and* 1½ inches from the left side.

A sailor who wants to give the location of his ship uses the same method. He gives two measurements. One is the distance north or south of the equator and

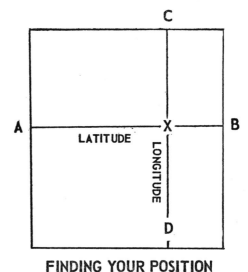

**FINDING YOUR POSITION
BY USE OF LATITUDE AND LONGITUDE**

is called the *latitude.* The other is the distance east or west of Greenwich, England and is called *longitude.* A line drawn through a given latitude and a line through a given longitude will cross at only *one* point on a map.

In order to find the exact spot to start the drawing in the diagram on page 50, *linear measure* is used. It deals with distances such as inches, feet, miles, and meters. Linear measure can be used on either flat or curved surfaces.

There is another way of measuring. It is called *ratio* and it shows us the relation of a part of something to the whole thing. If you fold a piece of paper exactly in the middle and then tear it, each piece is ½ of the whole sheet. If you fold one of the halves and tear it, each new piece is ¼ of the whole. If you tear a quarter, you will get pieces which are ⅛ of the whole. This can be continued through ¹⁄₁₆, ¹⁄₃₂, ¹⁄₆₄, and until the paper is smaller than confetti.

It is possible to divide a circle in the same way. But long ago the people of ancient Babylon (baa'-bih·lon) decided to divide the circle into 360 equal parts and today we still use their system. Each of these parts is called a *degree,* so there are 360 degrees in a circle. This is often written as 360°. The mark ° means degree. Each degree can be divided into 60 equal parts called *minutes,* written as 60'. And, if one wishes an even smaller measure, each minute can be

divided into 60 equal parts called *seconds,* written as
60″. For navigation purposes, generally only degrees
and minutes are used.

Man always has been very curious about this world
in which he lives. The people of ancient Greece were
unable to explore much of the surface of the earth because they had only very primitive means of travel.
They used their minds instead to find out things which
their eyes could never see. They invented *geometry*
(gee·om′eh·tree) to help them measure the earth. In
fact, the word geometry comes from two Greek words
which mean to measure the earth.

In order to locate a definite spot, it is necessary to
have not only two measurements, but also to know
where to start measuring. In the diagram on page 50
each measurement starts at a line that marks the edge
of the diagram. Any flat surface has a beginning and
an end, so it is always possible to find an edge from
which to start measuring. But look at a ball. There
is no beginning and no end, and our earth is shaped
roughly like a ball. When men decided to chart the
earth in terms of latitude and longitude, the first problem was where to begin.

To measure the earth, the people of ancient times
chose two imaginary lines. One is a straight line
running through the exact center of the earth from the
North Pole to the South Pole. This is called the
earth's axis. Of course they might have chosen an

imaginary line passing through the center of the earth in any direction, but because they knew that the stars seemed to wheel around a point in the sky directly above the earth's North Pole, it was logical for them to choose the north-south axis. Most globes of the earth are mounted on an axis which passes through the poles. But remember that the earth itself has no such real axis or poles; the axis of the earth is only an imaginary line around which the earth spins.

CUTOUT PORTION REPRESENTS ¼ or 90 DEGREES

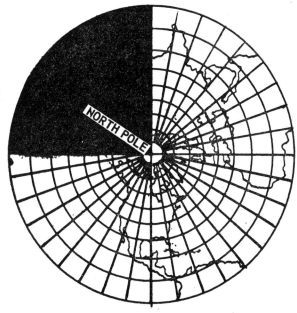

NORTH POLE

GLOBE IS 360 DEGREES

The second imaginary line they chose for measuring is a curved line which goes around the earth and is at all places halfway between the North and South Poles. This line is called the *equator* because it is equally distant from both poles, and divides the earth exactly in half. The distance from every point on the equator to either pole is one-fourth of a circle going completely around the earth and passing through each pole. Since a circle is divided into 360 degrees, the distance from the equator to either pole is one-fourth of 360 degrees or 90 degrees.

A position north of the equator is always written as so many degrees North Latitude, and south of the equator as so many degrees South Latitude. For example, Cocos Island, in the Pacific Ocean, is about 5 degrees north of the equator and is noted on sea charts as 5°30′ N. Lat. Easter Island is about 27 degrees south of the equator and is written as 27°3′ S. Lat.

When two or more lines are the same distance

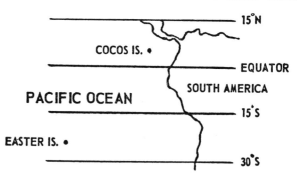

SHOWING POSITIONS OF COCOS AND EASTER ISLANDS

apart for their entire length, they are called parallel lines. On a globe you will find a number of circles which are parallel to the equator. These are *parallels of latitude.* Notice that as you come closer to the poles, the distance around each parallel becomes shorter. A parallel is a guide to help locate a spot on the globe.

If you want to find Bear Island, which is at 75° N. Lat. in the Arctic Ocean, you do not need to go all the

Globe showing parallels of latitude

way back to the equator to start measuring. You can look for it between the 70th and 80th parallels.

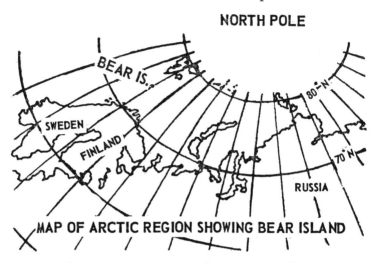

NORTH POLE

MAP OF ARCTIC REGION SHOWING BEAR ISLAND

A sailor at sea cannot reach out across the water to the imaginary line called the equator when he needs to measure the position of his ship. But just as he has learned to use the North Star to find direction, he can use it also to determine latitude. To understand the way in which the Pole Star helps a sailor, you must imagine that the part of the sky which can be seen from the Northern Hemisphere is like the inside of a great bowl hanging over the earth with the Pole Star at its center. The North Pole is almost directly under the North Star. (Actually, it is about 1 degree off center.)

As the earth spins around its axis, it appears as if the whole "bowl" of the sky is turning with only the

Pole Star standing still. If you hold a large salad bowl upside down over a globe of the earth, you will have a very rough model of the universe. Hold the center of the bowl directly over the pole and spin the globe slowly. It is easy to see that no matter where you stand in the Northern Hemisphere, except at the pole, the Pole Star will always be north of you.

When a sailor at sea looks into the distance in any direction, the earth and sky seem to be touching. As he slowly turns around, it seems as if the "bowl" of the sky meets the earth in a huge circle with him at the center. The circular line where earth and sky appear to meet is called the *horizon.* On the open sea, you can see the horizon very easily. You also can see parts of the horizon at the beach or any place on land where there are no hills or buildings to block your view.

Even before the time of Christ, people working with geometry found a way to measure latitude. They discovered that the angle formed by two imaginary lines, one from the horizon to the eye, the other from the eye to the Pole Star, was equal to the latitude. Of course a sailor cannot draw these imaginary lines, but he can do what the hunter does when he aims a gun. When a hunter lines up a rabbit in the sights of his rifle, he is drawing an imaginary line from his eye to the animal. In the same way, a sailor can "shoot" the Pole Star and the horizon. The size of the angle between these lines is roughly his latitude.

The nearer the sailor is to the equator, the smaller

VIEWS OF HORIZON

SAILOR AT SEA

STANDING ON A BEACH

LOCATED AT A HIGH POINT IN A CITY

58

★ NORTH STAR

SHOOTING THE HORIZON AND NORTH STAR

the angle between the imaginary lines. As a ship sails north the angle becomes larger. When a ship is off the coast of St. Augustine, Florida, the angle is 30 degrees and the latitude is 30 degrees North. If the ship sails north to White Bay, Newfoundland, the angle will then be 50 degrees and the latitude will be 50 degrees North.

A sailor can measure this angle by using a *sextant*. In its earliest form a sextant was simply two arms hinged together, one to sight the horizon and one to sight the star, and there was a scale to measure the angle between the arms. Because it is difficult to sight in two directions at the same time, the modern sextant was invented in 1731. This is a more com-

SEXTANTS

ANCIENT   MODERN

plicated instrument which uses a system of mirrors
and lenses on the arms so that the sailor can shoot the
star and the horizon at the same time. It also has a
more accurate scale.

Today the sailor can find his latitude more exactly
by correcting such known errors as the fact that the
Pole Star is about 1 degree off true north. He does
this quickly and easily by using one of the tables in the
Nautical Almanac, which is published each year by the
Naval Observatory in Washington, D.C.

You can find the latitude of your house by shooting
the North Star. Your results may not be absolutely accurate for many reasons. For one thing, you probably
will not have a sextant, but you can make a simple
angle measuring instrument, the *astrolabe* (as'tro-
labe). This is the instrument which was used by

sailors for several thousand years before the invention of the sextant.

NOW TRY THIS

You will need a straight piece of wood about 2 feet long, two screw eyes, a piece of string, a stone or other weight, a piece of adhesive tape, a thumbtack, and a protractor. A *protractor,* which is a half circle divided into 180 parts, or degrees, along its curve, is used to measure angles. (Remember, a complete circle has 360 degrees.) The picture below is a protractor. You may have a protractor, or you can buy one at a store that sells school supplies. If you want to make your own, trace the picture on very thin paper, paste it on cardboard, and cut around the outer line.

Fasten one screw eye into the top edge of the piece of wood about an inch from one end. Screw in the

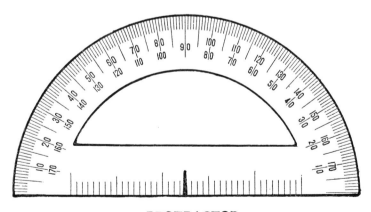

PROTRACTOR

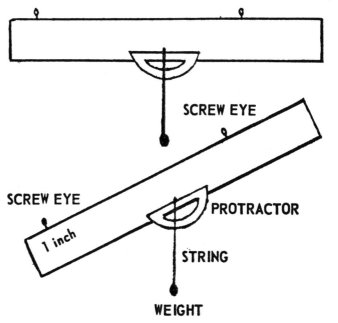

other about three-quarters of the way down the stick in a straight line with the first screw. These are your sights. Tape the protractor securely to the side of the wood. Be sure the straight edge of the protractor is parallel to the top edge of the wood. Tie one end of the string to the stone or weight. Attach the other end with a thumbtack to the wood directly above the arrow on the protractor. Now your astrolabe is ready for use. For best results, have a friend help you.

When the astrolabe is held level, the string will pass over the protractor at the 90-degree mark. In this position, the wood is pointing along the imaginary line from you to the horizon. Find the Pole Star in the night sky. (See page 18.) Now hold the end of the wood close to your eye and shoot the Pole Star by lining it up through the sights.

Be sure to keep your astrolabe steady in this position while your friend reads the degree mark where the weighted string crosses the circular scale on the protractor. This will give you a rough estimate of your latitude. Take turns shooting the star several times to get the most accurate reading possible. Parallels of latitude are numbered on the sides of a map. Check your results with the latitude of your home town as shown on a map.

People in the Southern Hemisphere cannot find latitude by a pole star. Because of the curve of the

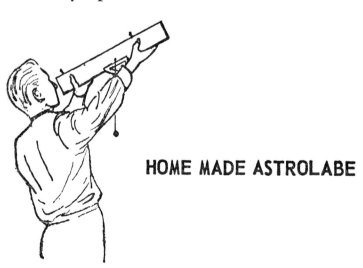

HOME MADE ASTROLABE

earth, the Pole Star cannot be seen below the equator, and there is no star directly over the South Pole. However, the *Nautical Almanac* has tables which can be used to find latitude by shooting other stars, including the sun.

5. Mapping the Sea: Finding the Longitude

A sailor who knows only that a ship's latitude is 30 degrees North is in the same position as you were when you wanted to meet your friend on Main Street. Just as your friend might be anywhere along Main Street, so the ship might be 30 degrees north of the equator anywhere around the earth. You needed to know where on Main Street your friend was waiting, and the sailor must know the longitude if he wishes to find the exact location of the ship.

A line of longitude, or a *meridian* (muh·rid'ee·an) is a half circle running across the earth from the North Pole to the South Pole. In order to measure distance, there must be a starting place. Choosing a starting place to measure latitude was easy. Parallels of latitude become smaller as they approach the poles, and the largest parallel, the equator, is exactly halfway between the poles. There is no such natural starting place for longitude. All the meridians are the same length. And, since there are no east-west poles, there can be no mid-point. But 45 degrees West Longitude has no meaning unless you know west of what, and so map makers have had to choose a fixed starting place or *prime meridian.*

Of course, each country wanted the honor of having its capital located on the prime meridian. There are old maps which show the prime meridian passing through Paris, Rome, Washington, and many other cities. On English maps, it passes through the Greenwich Observatory in southwest London. This was confusing enough in olden days, but imagine what would happen if we still used all these cities. When the *Titanic* radioed its position as 50°14′ W. Long. only another English ship would have located it correctly. A French ship would have searched the ocean 60 miles east of the accident because Paris is 60 miles east of London; an Italian ship would have looked for the *Titanic* 500 miles east of its location; while a ship using American charts would have hurried to a spot in the Pacific Ocean off the west coast of Canada.

As England became the most important sea power, more and more maps were made in London. These were so good that they were used by sailors of many nations. Since English maps measured longitude from the Greenwich meridian, it came to be widely used as the prime meridian, and, in 1884, most of the countries of the world agreed to accept it. All places along this meridian from the North to the South Pole are located at 0 degrees Longitude. Places west of the prime meridian are measured in degrees west, for example, New York City is 74° West Longitude. Places east of the Greenwich meridian are measured in degrees east. Berlin is 13° 25′ East Longitude.

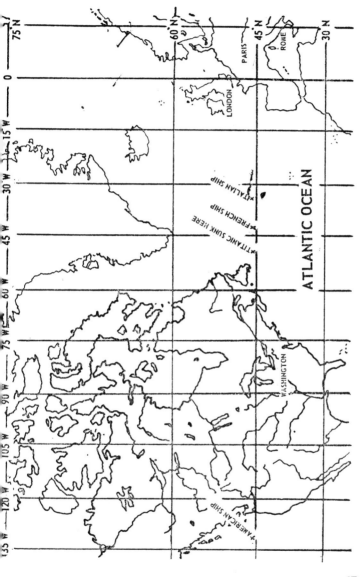

ATLANTIC OCEAN

TITANIC SUNK HERE

FRENCH SHIP

ITALIAN SHIP

AMERICAN SHIP

WASHINGTON

LONDON

PARIS

ROME

75 N

60 N

45 N

30 N

135 W   120 W   105 W   90 W   75 W   60 W   45 W   30 W   15 W   0

67

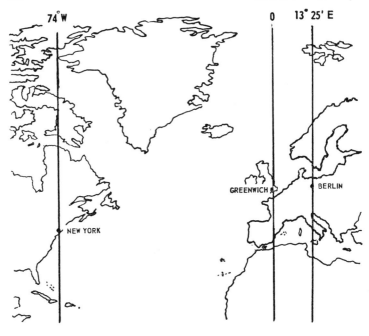

It is simple enough to find the longitude of a city on a map because the meridians are drawn and the degrees of longitude are printed across the top and bottom. But a sailor far at sea cannot find his longitude so easily. There are no cities or other visible landmarks on the trackless ocean. Just as he looks to the skies to find his latitude, a sailor can determine his longitude from the sun and the stars.

The men who lived in ancient times learned many things about the earth from studying the heavens. Since the appearance of the sun in the sky divided day from night, it was natural for them to measure time according to the position of the sun. Time measured this way is called *Solar Time*.

If you chart the position of the sun for one day, it seems to cross the sky in a great half circle, rising out of the eastern horizon at dawn and sinking below the western horizon at dusk. The highest point in this circle is called the *zenith*. When the sun reaches its zenith, it is noon Solar Time.

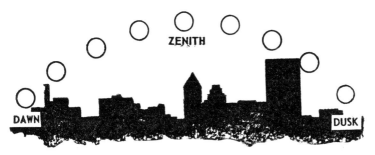

PATH OF THE SUN DURING A DAY

NOW TRY THIS

It is, of course, the earth spinning around its axis which makes the sun appear to move across the "bowl" of the sky. Hold a flashlight to represent the sun several feet from a globe of the earth. It is noon all along the meridian which passes through the center of the beam of light. Now turn the globe slowly from west to east. This is the direction in which the earth spins. You can see that it is noon along only one meridian at a time and that as the earth turns, noon occurs farther and farther west.

Noon in Chicago comes after it occurs in New York, and noon in San Francisco comes after noon in Chicago. In one hour the earth turns ½₄ of a complete circle. Since there are 360 degrees in a circle, we know that with the passing of each hour the zenith of the sun will be over a meridian that is ½₄ of 360 degrees, or 15 degrees, farther west.

The sailor can use the spinning of the earth to measure longitude. By shooting the sun with his sextant, he can find the exact moment when the sun reaches its zenith. This is noon Solar Time all along the meridian on which his ship is located. He can compare this with Greenwich Time, which is Solar Time along the prime meridian and is often written as G.T.

Each hour before noon Greenwich Time is equal to 15° East Longitude, and each hour after noon Greenwich Time means 15° West Longitude. When it is noon on a ship at sea, while back in Greenwich it is one o'clock, the ship's longitude is 15° West. If it is 3:30 G.T., the ship's longitude is three-and-a-half times 15 degrees, or 52° 30′ West. At 11:00 G.T., the ship's longitude is 15° East, and earlier in the morning, at 8:30 G.T., the ship would be located somewhere along the meridian of 52° 30′ East Longitude. At night, the sailor can shoot the stars and then use the tables in the *Nautical Almanac* to find his longitude.

Even in ancient times, men knew that longitude could be measured by comparing Solar Time with the

time at the prime meridian. Unfortunately, this fact
was of no use to a sailor until he had an accurate way
of always knowing what time it was at the prime meridian. The earliest timepieces, such as the sundial
and the hourglass, could not help him. Although some
clocks were in use before the time of Columbus, these
were tremendous weight-driven machines, each of
which needed a whole tower for its case. By the early
1500s watches known as Nuremberg Eggs were being
used. Unfortunately, these were often wrong by as
much as sixteen minutes a day. Since four minutes of
time is equal to 1 degree of longitude, by the end of
a day, a ship using such a watch might be as much as
4 degrees from its correct position. At the equator this
could be 276½ miles.

Although there was no scientific method of finding
the longitude of a ship, great voyages of discovery were
made during the fifteenth, sixteenth, and seventeenth
centuries. These explorers used a method of navigation which is called *dead reckoning*. The sailor keeps
a record of how far and in what direction his ship has
traveled. Because he knows how many miles there
are in a degree, he has a good idea of the location of his
ship. Columbus used dead reckoning when he sailed
from Spain in 1492. In later voyages, he was able to
sail directly to the same islands by use of this system.

Columbus, like all skilled navigators, knew the importance of keeping accurate records. Even today
dead reckoning is used. At regular intervals, the navi-

gator uses a plotting sheet prepared by the U.S. Hydrographic Office to mark the path of the ship and the distance it has traveled. This helps him to see at a glance the approximate location of his ship.

But in the stormy seas of the North Atlantic it is often difficult to keep a ship on an exact course and to determine distance correctly. An error of a few miles might mean little in the middle of the ocean, but this same error could wreck a ship as it approaches a fogbound coast. Because of her great sea trade, England had to find an accurate way of determining longitude.

In 1714, the "Commissioners for the Discovery of Longitude at Sea" offered a prize of about $100,000 to anyone who could solve the problem. The prize was won, not by a great scientist or scholar, but by a Yorkshire carpenter, John Harrison, who invented the *chronometer* (cro·nom′eh·ter). This is a very accurate watch which is not affected by the pitching and rolling of the ship. It is set to Greenwich Time and no matter where in the world a sailor is, he only needs to look at the chronometer to find the exact time along the prime meridian.

On modern ships, the chronometer and the compass are considered equal in importance as instruments of navigation. The care of the chronometer is the responsibility of one crew member throughout the voyage. Although it can run for fifty-six hours between windings, the rule is that this crew member must wind it every twenty-four hours and then report to the captain that the chronometer has been wound. As an additional safety measure, large ships often carry several chronometers.

Most watches are not set to Solar Time. Since the earth is constantly spinning, the longitudinal line along which it is noon is always changing. For this reason, Solar Time cannot be used conveniently for everyday purposes. Imagine the confusion there would be if watches were set by Solar Time. Time would change whenever you traveled a few miles east or west. When it is twelve o'clock at Beaumont, in eastern Texas, it is 11:11 Solar Time in El Paso, on the western border of

MAP OF TEXAS SHOWING SOLAR TIME

the state; and each city along the way has a different Solar Time.

To avoid such confusion, the world has been divided into time zones. A time zone covers roughly 15 degrees of longitude. Standard Civil Time for the entire zone is the same as Solar Time along the meridian which runs through the center of the time zone. Each time zone extends from the North Pole to the South Pole. Rio de Janeiro is in the same time zone as Godthaab, Greenland; Lima, Peru, and New York City are in the same zone; and Cape Town, South Africa, has the same Standard Civil Time as Moscow, U.S.S.R.

When it is 3 A.M. in San Francisco, it is 6 A.M. in New York, and 12 noon at Greenwich. Halfway around the world from Greenwich, along the 180th meridian, it is midnight. The 180th meridian is called the *International Date Line,* for when it is one minute after 12 noon on Monday in Greenwich, on the 180th meridian it is one minute after 12 midnight, and therefore it is already Tuesday. If a great circle is drawn around the earth, passing through both poles and through Greenwich, England, one half of the circle is the prime meridian and the other half is the International Date Line. The longitude of the International Date Line can be written either 180° East or 180° West, since it is equally distant from the prime meridian in either direction.

Dividing the time zones along the meridians works very well at sea. Unfortunately for this system, when

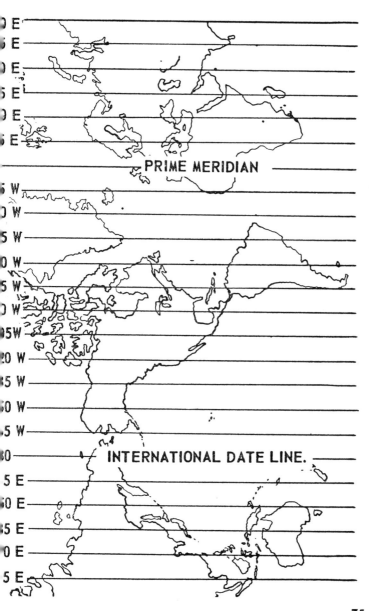

0 E
5 E
0 E
5 E
0 E
5 E

PRIME MERIDIAN

5 W
0 W
5 W
0 W
5 W
0 W
05W
20 W
35 W
50 W
5 W

80

INTERNATIONAL DATE LINE.

5 E
60 E
35 E
0 E
5 E

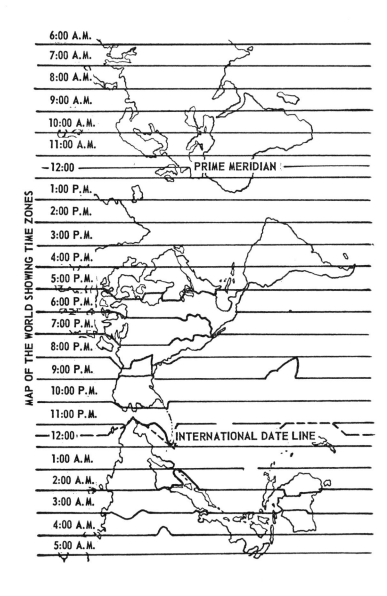

6:00 A.M.
7:00 A.M.
8:00 A.M.
9:00 A.M.
10:00 A.M.
11:00 A.M.
—12:00 —————————— PRIME MERIDIAN —————
1:00 P.M.
2:00 P.M.
3:00 P.M.
4:00 P.M.
5:00 P.M.
6:00 P.M.
7:00 P.M.
8:00 P.M.
9:00 P.M.
10:00 P.M.
11:00 P.M.
—12:00 —————— INTERNATIONAL DATE LINE —————
1:00 A.M.
2:00 A.M.
3:00 A.M.
4:00 A.M.
5:00 A.M.

MAP OF THE WORLD SHOWING TIME ZONES

INTERNATIONAL DATE LINE.   **PRIME MERIDIAN**

men built cities they were not thinking about meridians. As a result, such cities as Wichita, Kansas, Butte, Montana, and Sarasota, Florida, would lie in two time zones. This would make life very difficult. It would be even more difficult on islands which are cut by the meridian of the International Date Line. For convenience, time zones on land do not always follow the meridians exactly.

NOW TRY THIS

You can use Solar Time to find the longitude of your house. Even if you do not have a sextant, there is an easy way to determine when it is noon Solar Time. You will need two pencils, a sheet of paper, a cork or an eraser, a watch set accurately by radio time, and a sunny day. About 11:00 A.M. (if you are on Daylight Saving Time, start at twelve o'clock) place the paper in the sun on a flat surface such as a sidewalk. Be sure to choose an out-of-the-way place as the paper must

TIME ZONES OF THE UNITED STATES

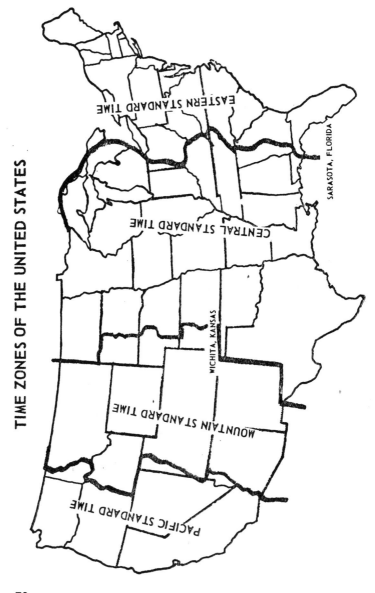

EASTERN STANDARD TIME

CENTRAL STANDARD TIME

MOUNTAIN STANDARD TIME

PACIFIC STANDARD TIME

SARASOTA, FLORIDA

WICHITA, KANSAS

not be moved until the experiment is finished. If it is windy, anchor the paper firmly with something heavy. Push the pencil into the eraser or cork so that it will stand straight up. Place the pencil so that it casts a shadow on the paper. With another pencil mark the end of the shadow on the paper and note the exact time. Mark the shadow end and time every five minutes.

In the diagram you can see what happens to the shadow of the pencil as the sun approaches its zenith. When the sun is at its highest point, the pencil shadow is shortest, and it is noon Solar Time. Even the ancient people knew that the shortest shadow occurs at noon.

You probably have no chronometer to tell you Greenwich Time, but if your watch is set accurately and you know the time zone in which you live, you can find Greenwich Time by using the next table.

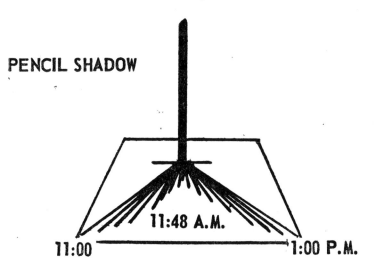

PENCIL SHADOW

11:48 A.M.

11:00   1:00 P.M.

TABLE FOR FINDING GREENWICH TIME

Time Zone	*Greenwich Time*
Atlantic Standard Time	add 4 hours
Atlantic "Summer" Time	add 5 hours
Eastern Standard Time	add 5 hours
Eastern Daylight Time	add 6 hours
Central Standard Time	add 6 hours
Central Daylight Time	add 7 hours
Mountain Standard Time	add 7 hours
Mountain Daylight Time	add 8 hours
Pacific Standard Time	add 8 hours
Pacific Daylight Time	add 9 hours

Suppose you live in Bowling Green, Indiana, and you find that noon Solar Time occurs at 11:48 A.M. Central Standard Time. To find Greenwich Time, you add six hours. The time back in Greenwich would be 11:48 plus six hours or 5:48 P.M.

Noon occurs four minutes later for each degree you travel farther west. If you know the difference in minutes between local noon Solar Time and the time at the prime meridian, you can divide this number by four to find your longitude. In Bowling Green, the difference between noon and Greenwich Time is five hours and forty-eight minutes. Since there are sixty minutes in an hour, in five hours there are 300 minutes and in 5:48 there are 348 minutes. Three hundred forty-eight divided by four equals eighty-seven. Because the Central Time Zone is west of the prime meridian, the longitude of Bowling Green is 87° West.

The meridians of longitude are numbered on the

top and bottom of a map. After you have worked out your longitude, compare your answer with the longitude of your town as shown on a map. It is possible you may find an error of a few degrees. Remember that each four minutes noon occurs one degree westward. If your watch is not set accurately, or if you do not observe the exact minute when the pencil's shadow is shortest, there will be an error. For best results, repeat this experiment on several sunny days.

Knowing how to find the latitude and longitude gives the sailor his "address" at sea. With his plotting sheets and this knowledge, he can guide his ship across the trackless waste from Land's End, England, to within sight of the Statue of Liberty. But this information is not enough to bring him safely to his pier in New York Harbor. More charts are needed.

6. Mapping the Sea: Navigation Charts

Sea charts showing the latitude and longitude of the land masses are the road maps of the ocean. But many other types of charts are needed to ensure a safe voyage. Of great importance are the pilot charts. These are carefully marked to show the depth of the water.

Although the bottom is called the floor of the ocean, it is unlike any floor you have ever seen. Rising from the ocean bottom are mountain peaks taller than most mountains on dry land, and yet they do not break the surface of the water. The tallest mountain in the world is not Mt. Everest, which is only 29,142 feet, it is Mauna Kea in Hawaii, which rises 31,000 feet from the floor of the Pacific Ocean. But only the top 13,823 feet can be seen above the water. The sea has canyons which are deeper and more beautiful than Grand Canyon. Cliffs almost 5 miles high rise in the middle of the Atlantic and yet they are still hidden by a mile of water.

Under a ship the ocean floor may have a rug of gently rippling sand. It may be strewn with huge boulders or be covered with many feet of thick, slimy ooze. The depth of the ocean ranges from its shores, which are covered only at high tide, to the Challenger Deep near the Island of Guam in the Pacific, where it goes down almost 7 miles.

Charts of the ocean bottom are part of the equipment of every ship. Even though it is made of strongest steel, a ship will not last long if it is pounded against a reef. A ship stuck on a sand bar is of no use to its owners. Maps warn the sailor of such dangers ahead.

The peaks, deeps, and reefs also serve as landmarks. Just as you use mountain peaks and rivers on land, the sailor can check his location by comparing the pattern of the ocean floor with his charts. On land only your eyes are needed to find landmarks, but the sailor needs more than his eyes to find the landmarks of the ocean floor. He must take *soundings*. The oldest and simplest device is the *hand lead*. This is a lead cone with an eye in the top to which the line is attached. In the bottom is a hole which can be filled with tallow or grease whenever a sample of the ocean bed is needed. When the lead touches bottom, bits of the sea floor stick to the grease.

The line on the hand lead is usually made of braided flax. It is marked in *fathoms*. One fathom equals six feet. Since the line is often used at night, it has markers so that the sailor can "read" the line by feel. Standard markers are shown on the next page.

As a sailor "reads" the line, he calls out, "By the mark three," "By the mark five," or whatever depth he finds. The famous American writer, Samuel Clemens, who often sailed on the Mississippi River boats, chose his pen name from the 2-fathom report of the sailors who manned the hand leads, "By the mark twain."

Fathoms	Markers
2	2 strips of leather
3	3 strips of leather
5	white cotton rag
10	piece of leather with a hole in it
20	a cord with 2 knots
25	a cord with 1 knot
30	a cord with 3 knots
35	a cord with 1 knot
40	a cord with 4 knots
45	a cord with 1 knot

For deep-sea soundings the *dipsey lead* can be used. This may weigh from 30 to 100 pounds, and its line is made of piano wire. In very deep water, it takes several hours to make one sounding by this method. For this reason, the dipsey lead is seldom used today. Modern ships use a *fathometer*. This is an electrical device which sends a ping of sound down through the water. When the sound strikes the ocean floor, the echo bounces back to the ship. The fathometer keeps an accurate record of the length of time it takes the sound to travel down and back. Sound travels about 800 fathoms each second. If it takes one second for the ping to reach bottom and return, the depth of the ocean floor is one-half of 800 fathoms, or 400 fathoms. With a fathometer it takes only 6.6 seconds to measure a depth of 3 miles; 3.3 seconds to travel 3 miles down and 3.3 seconds to travel 3 miles back to the ship. Imagine lowering a 100-pound dipsey lead on 3 miles of piano wire!

Pilot charts of the North Atlantic, North Pacific, Indian Ocean, and Central American waters are published each month by the U.S. Hydrographic Office. Charts of the South Atlantic and South Pacific are published four times a year. New charts must be made available regularly, because in addition to information about depths and soundings, these indicate the winds and currents that can be expected.

Currents move through the ocean in somewhat the same way as rivers and streams move across the land. The drops of water which wash the ocean beach this year are not the same drops which splashed there a year ago. Some of the water in which you swim may once have sparkled on the beaches of tropical islands. Other drops may have helped to float icebergs as they slipped from the glaciers of Greenland. The waters of the ocean are never still. They are being mixed and churned constantly by the swiftly moving currents. Because the course of the currents is more or less fixed, they can be shown on charts.

The currents of the ocean are created by many different forces. The winds constantly blowing over the surface, the changing temperatures and the differences in saltiness of the waters all play a part. Certainly you have noticed the difference in temperature of the air in a room. On the floor you may feel cool, but if you climb a step ladder so that your head is near the ceiling, you will feel much warmer. Cold air is heavier than warm air, and cold water is heavier than warm water. Icy water from the Arctic and Antarctic regions slips downward into the ocean depths, while water from the seas near the equator forms the warm currents which flow at the surface. In the same way, the heavy, saltier water from the Mediterranean Sea sinks to the bottom and flows into the Atlantic deeps, while a current of lighter, less salty water floods back to take its place.

There is a two-way traffic of more salty and less

ATLANTIC MAIN OCEAN CURRENTS

salty water passing through the Strait of Gibraltar. During the Second World War, German submarines used these currents to help them sneak past the guns of the British fort at Gibraltar. With their engines dead, they slithered in with the less salty upper current, and out again in the saltier lower current.

Regular ships also need information about the currents. Unless the sailor is prepared, strong and tricky currents in harbors and along the shores can quickly

PACIFIC MAIN OCEAN CURRENTS

wreck his ship. Powerful ocean-going currents such as the Gulf Stream help the sailor by speeding his ship across the ocean. The regular shipping lanes used by most ocean traffic depend on the currents. Because currents change at different times of the year, new pilot charts must be issued regularly.

Recently a new aid to navigation was worked out, and with it came a new kind of chart. The aid is called *loran,* short for LOng RAnge Navigation. There is a series of curves printed on one side and a chart of the ocean on the other. Loran stations, which are radio sending stations, have been built along most of the important coast lines of the world. A loran station is made up of one master and two slave units, each of which sends out radio signals.

A receiving set on board ship measures the difference in the length of time it takes for the radio signals to travel from each of the units of a single loran station to the ship. There is one curve, and only one curve, on the loran chart for each time difference. When this curve has been found, the receiving set is tuned to another loran station and again the time difference is measured. The ship's position is the point where the curve of the second station crosses the curve of the first station. With loran, a sailor can find his position in a few minutes almost as accurately as he can by shooting the sun or stars.

7. Mapping the Sky: Man Among the Stars

Wherever men travel they make paths for others to follow. Everyone on earth has used some kind of road during his life. Whether they are made of dirt, macadam, or concrete, the land roads form a network across the face of the earth. Roads do not wind aimlessly, even though sometimes it seems so. They are built to connect the places which are important to men, and they twist and turn in order to avoid such obstacles as hills, cliffs, and rivers.

Perhaps it is difficult to imagine roads on the sea. Although there are no strips of concrete stretching across the ocean waters, there are roads. The roads of the sea are the shipping lanes. These lanes connect the coastal cities of the world. Shipping lanes are more direct than land roads because there are no hills, cliffs, or rivers in the way. The path of a sea road depends on the ocean currents, the winds, the weather, and such obstacles as reefs and icebergs.

There are also roads in the sky. These are not built with millions of tons of concrete. Instead, they are paved with invisible radio beams. Perhaps you live under a sky road. If each day at the same time, planes traveling in the same general direction pass over your house, you can be sure there is an *airway* over your head. Airways connect the cities of the world. They are usually very direct, but they do depend in part on the winds, the weather, and the presence of emergency landing fields.

In the early days of the airplane, there were no roads in the air. Even after the airplane proved its military value during the First World War, there were only a few planes in use. Most of these were used to amuse people at carnivals and country fairs. A pilot could take off from any large, smooth field, fly in any direction he pleased, and land wherever he wished. The air was a trackless frontier like the wilderness that faced the early American pioneers.

At first, the pilots used a system of navigation called *contact flying*. The flyer found his way across the countryside by following landmarks. Contact flying is like the church steeple navigation of the Middle Ages. The pilot must have clear daylight and must remain within sight of familiar landmarks. Today, a contact flight is known as V.F.R., visual flight rules.

The earliest pilots used automobile road maps and U.S. Coast and Geodetic Survey maps for contact flights. Villages, rivers, and especially railroad tracks were used as guides. This worked very well during the day, but at night all planes had to be grounded. As long as planes were used mainly for amusement, night flying was unimportant, but in 1920 the U.S. Government decided to start transcontinental air-mail service.

At first, air mail was flown only from dawn to dusk. At the end of the day, the plane landed and the mail was loaded onto a train. All through the night the mail sacks traveled on land; then, the next morning, they were transferred to a plane and continued their trip by air. A letter using this service crossed the country twenty-two hours faster.

After one year of this plane-train service, the U.S. Post Office decided it wanted an all-plane service. Some kind of beacon was needed to guide the plane at night. For the first flight, farmers helped by lighting bonfires along the way. Because this flight was a success, Congress voted to spend the money to build flashing beacons to mark the airways of the United States. Since a beacon has little value unless a pilot knows where it is located, the U.S. Coast and Geodetic Survey began to print *Sectional Aeronautical Charts*. These show the locations of airports, beacons, and other guides to air navigation.

Modern American airways are made of radio beams. At regular intervals along the way, radio transmitting stations send out constant signals in certain directions. One antenna sends the International Code for "*A*" (dot-dash) while another sends the code for "*N*" (dash-dot). Together these signals form a broad beam. The receiving set of a plane flying down one side of a beam will receive only dash-dot. A plane on the opposite side will receive only dot-dash, but a plane in the center will receive both signals. A mix-

SYMBOLS USED ON AERONAUTICAL CHARTS

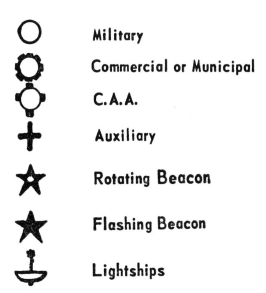

Military

Commercial or Municipal

C.A.A.

Auxiliary

Rotating Beacon

Flashing Beacon

Lightships

ture of dot-dash and dash-dot sounds like a constant hum. When a pilot hears this hum in his ear phones, he knows he is "on the beam," and headed straight for his destination.

The beams of *radio range courses* are marked in purple on Sectional Aeronautical Charts. Radio beams fan out as they pass through the air. The farther the beam is from the station, the wider the area it covers. For this reason, the beam is shown on the chart as a giant pointer. The compass directions are marked in degrees on each beam, and each chart has several compass roses for convenience.

The circle of a compass rose, or the card of the com-

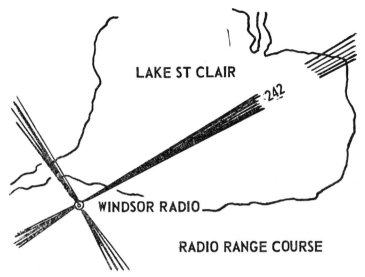

LAKE ST CLAIR

242

WINDSOR RADIO

RADIO RANGE COURSE

pass itself, may be marked in two ways. It may be divided into 360 degrees as on the Sectional Charts. This makes it possible to measure direction very accurately. Or like early compasses, it may be divided into thirty-two points, each named for a direction. For example, the points between North and East are:

> North
> North by East
> North North East
> North East by North
> North East
> North East by East
> East North East
> East by North
> East

When you have learned the points all the way around, you can "box the compass." Today many compass cards are marked in both degrees and points.

The greatest advantage of airplane travel is speed. Even before the invention of the airplane, men had learned how to travel faster on land. A crack train, for example, can speed along at more than 90 miles per hour. Ocean travel, however, has always been slower, and ocean distances are greater. Even today,

COMPASS CARD

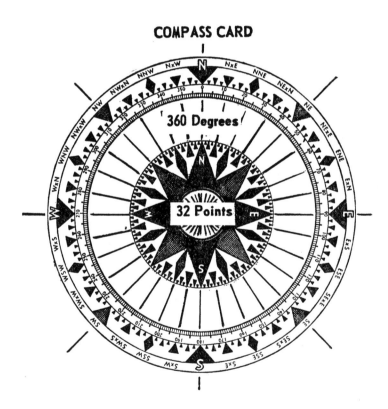

the fastest luxury liner does not average 30 miles per hour. But 30 miles an hour is very slow, and it still takes more than four days to cross the Atlantic by ship.

With the first successful flight, people began to dream of using aircraft to span the ocean. But it was many years before this dream could come true. It is much more difficult to plot a plane course over the water than over the land. Contact flying is impossible for there are no visible landmarks. Moreover, a plane must often fly through heavy fog or at night. It certainly would not be practical to try to build a string of beacons across the ocean.

There are so many problems involved in airplane navigation over water that many people believed it would never be possible. In fact, when a London newspaper, the *Daily Mail,* offered a prize of about $5,000 to anyone who could fly across the English Channel, many people thought it was cheap publicity. After all, even at its narrowest point, it is 21 miles across the Channel between England and France. How could a plane possibly fly such a distance!

But, in 1909, Blériot did succeed in crossing the foggy Channel, and fliers continued to dream of crossing the ocean. When Lindbergh planned to cross the Atlantic in 1927, he purchased regular ship charts from a ship-chandler's shop at San Pedro, California. In addition to maps showing latitude, longitude, and land masses, he bought a time-zone chart and weather maps. Once, as he was flying over Nova Scotia on his way to Paris, the wind caught a corner of a map and fluttered it toward a window. He grabbed it back quickly, for if it had blown away, he would have been forced to return to New York. He was flying on course; his plane was in excellent condition; he had enough gas; but, without his chart, he never could have reached Paris.

Like Columbus, Lindbergh steered his way across the ocean by dead reckoning. He followed the course marked on a ship's chart, using only compasses to indicate the direction and the plane's speedometer to help him estimate the distance. Since he flew alone, he had to check the course as well as handle the controls of the plane. The airplanes that fly the oceans today always have a navigator who is responsible for plotting the route and seeing that the plane remains on course.

The airplane navigator, like the ship navigator, depends on dead reckoning, radio, and the stars. It may seem strange, but the men who guide our most modern means of transportation depend in part on the oldest science in the world, *astronomy*, the study of the stars. Star charts were among the first maps made.

Look up into the night sky and pick out a star. It seems to be only a twinkle of light in a diamond-studded sky. Because the earth is spinning, the stars, like the sun, never seem to stay in the same place. Each hour and each day your special star will appear in a different spot. If you want to study this star, you must have a sure way of locating it each night.

One way to find a star in the heavens or on a chart was worked out by the people of the ancient world. Just as you sometimes can see animals or faces in the clouds, they pictured figures outlined by the stars. To each of these groups of stars or *constellations,* they gave the name of an imaginary hero or an animal, and they made up wonderful legends about them.

Different tribes saw different pictures in the stars. The people of ancient Greece made charts showing forty-eight constellations. These are still used on the star charts of the Northern Hemisphere. Suppose the star which you chose is the first one in the pointer of the Big Dipper sometimes called Ursa Major. You can locate this star, which the Arabian astronomers named *Dubhe,* by first finding the Big Dipper. This is like finding a country on a map when you know on which continent it is located.

NOW TRY THIS

You can plot the course of Dubhe across the heavens. On paper, draw a large circle to represent the "bowl" of the sky. Mark the Pole Star, sometimes called Polaris, in the center of the circle and draw a line from the horizon (the edge of the paper) to the Pole Star. To orient your map, be sure that this line

is pointing north each time you chart the position of the star. Now pick out Dubhe in the night sky and mark its position in the circle. Once each week at the same hour, mark its position on your chart. In three months, Dubhe will have traveled one-fourth of the way around Polaris. In six months it will be halfway around. And if you continue for a whole year, you will find that Dubhe is right back where it started.

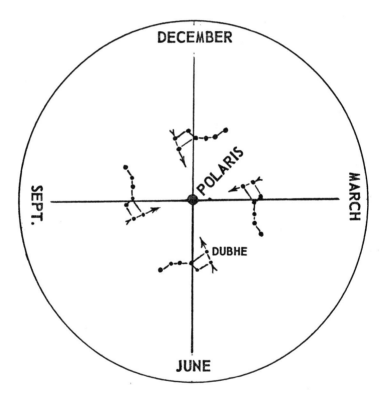

CHART SHOWING PATH OF DUBHE AROUND POLARIS

Today there are other ways to locate stars. If the latitude and longitude of a ship at sea is known, it can be pin-pointed without difficulty. A similar system has been worked out for the sky. Just as there are imaginary poles and an equator on earth, there are imaginary poles and an equator on the "bowl" of the sky. The North Star, Polaris, is just 1 degree from the imaginary north pole. Latitude on the "bowl" of the sky is called *declination* (deck'lin·ay"shun) and longitude is *right ascension* (as·en'shun). Like latitude and longitude on earth, these may be measured in degrees. The declination of Dubhe is 63 degrees and its right ascension is 175 degrees. If you know the declination and right ascension of a star you can find it on a chart or in the sky even if it is not part of a constellation. This is important today since we have discovered many stars which can be seen only with a powerful telescope.

A very interesting type of star chart is one with a movable center card or wheel. By turning this, it is possible to see exactly which stars are overhead at each hour of each day and night of the year. Some of these charts show declination and right ascension as well as the constellations.

The positions of the planets are not shown on the movable wheel charts. The astronomers of the ancient world noticed that some heavenly bodies did not stay in a fixed place as the stars wheeled around. They named them *planets* from the Greek word meaning wanderer, since they wandered in and out among the

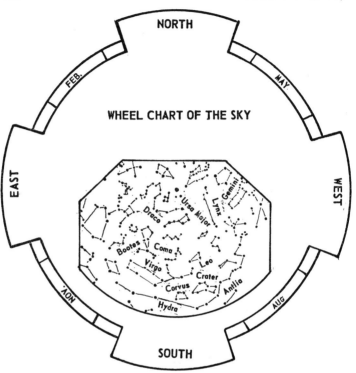

stars during the course of the year. Today we know
that they are not stars at all, but are parts of the Solar
System like our earth. The planets follow a definite
path as they revolve around the sun. The *ecliptic,*
the great circle path which they seem to follow through
the sky, is often marked on charts. Tables which give
the declination and right ascension of the planets for
each day of each year make it possible for you to locate
them on the ecliptic.

Astronomers even have mapped the surface of one of the planets. Maps of Mars show the positions of the polar caps and the dark areas where it is thought vegetation may be growing. By comparing old maps and photographs with those made recently, the astronomers learned that a new dark area about the size of Texas has appeared in what was believed to be a desert. An interesting early map of Mars was prepared by

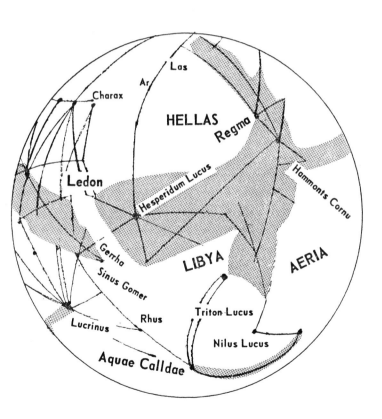

Professor Percival Lowell, founder of the Lowell Observatory in Flagstaff, Arizona. This map shows the lines or canals which some astronomers have seen on Mars. Professor Lowell suggested that these are irrigation ditches made by intelligent beings. This theory is not accepted generally by present-day scientists.

There are many charts of the moon, which is the earth's only natural satellite. A *satellite* is a small body which revolves around a planet. Moon charts show the positions of the craters, mountains, and lunar seas. Lunar seas are not seas in the ordinary sense of the word since there is no water on the moon. They are the dark patches which seem to form the face of the "man in the moon."

The moon plays a most important role in the mapping of the earth. Just as map makers learned to use mountain tops to measure distances on the continents by triangulation, they now have worked out a way to use the moon as one corner of a triangle to measure the distances between continents. This method was worked out for use during the International Geophysical Year of 1957–1958.

Some of the most important information about the earth and the universe has been learned during the International Years. These began with the First International Polar Year held in 1882–1883. At that time, bases were set up in the Arctic and much was learned about the northern lights, the earth's magnetism, and the weather. The Second International Polar Year was fifty years later, in 1932–1933. It supplied much new knowledge which was used to improve radio communication and to develop radar.

These International Years were so successful that the nations agreed to have one every fifty years. But science advanced so fast that they could wait only twenty-five years. The Third International Year, known as the International Geophysical Year, was called for 1957–1958. The latest International Year is by far the most ambitious. It involves many countries working together and sharing information for the benefit of all.

Once again the earth's magnetism needed to be studied since its constant changes cause errors in compass readings, sometimes making the needle point far from true north. Even though scientists are not sure why the compass varies, they have been able to map its *deviations* for all parts of the earth. These maps have to be redrawn often because the earth's magnetism is constantly changing.

Although the International Geophysical Year is known most widely for its work on artificial satellites, another of the main purposes is the same as that of the First International Polar Year: to increase man's knowledge of the weather. Charles Dudley Warner once wrote, "Everyone talks about the weather, but nobody does anything about it." People thought that was a joke in 1890, but today only the first part, "Everyone talks about the weather," is true.

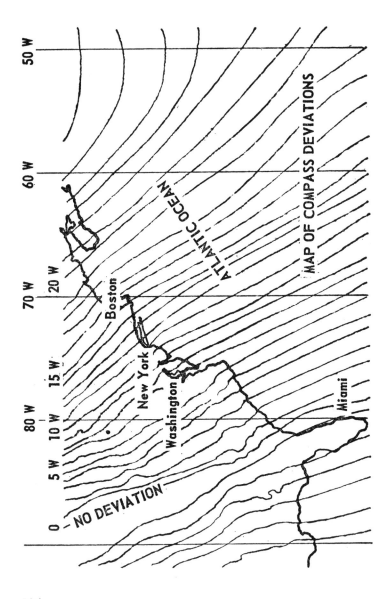

8. Mapping the Sky: Weather

Perhaps one reason everyone talks about the weather is because it is ever changing. Within a twenty-four-hour period it is possible to have rain, sun, wind, calm, and a 20-degree change of temperature. For this reason, weather maps are printed daily in many newspapers. Land maps often can be used for many years, pilot charts are issued once a month, but new weather maps are made several times a day.

Weather seemed very mysterious to primitive people. Even during the Middle Ages, great storms were looked upon as punishment for evil deeds, or perhaps the work of a witch. The first attempt at scientific prediction of the weather came as a result of the invention of the *barometer* in 1643 by Torricelli, an Italian scientist.

The barometer is a device which measures the pressure of the air. A Torricelli barometer can be made by filling a narrow glass tube about 34 inches long with mercury. The tube is turned upside down and placed in a bowl full of mercury. To be sure that no air can bubble up through the mercury, the mouth of the tube is covered while it is being turned. Under normal conditions, the liquid metal in the tube will drop until it stands at about 30 inches above the surface of the mercury in the bowl.

When the air is heavier, its pressure on the mercury in the bowl is greater and the mercury is forced higher into the tube. When this happens, we say, "The barometer is rising." When the air is lighter, there is less pressure on the mercury in the bowl and the mercury in the tube drops lower. Then we say, "The barometer is falling." It did not take long to discover that bad weather often follows a falling barometer.

Weather is an international problem and men from many countries have added to our knowledge. Professor Brande of Breslau University in Poland made one of the greatest contributions. He decided to make charts showing weather changes over a large part of Europe during the year 1783. Generally, a map maker draws a map so that he can share his knowledge with others quickly and easily. In this case, the map maker himself gained a great deal of knowledge by drawing his map.

There was no radio, telephone, or telegraph to help him, so Brande slowly collected his information by mail. As he drew the charts, he noticed that local storms were often part of larger storm systems. Many of these storm systems followed the same general path as they moved across Europe.

The knowledge gained from these early charts was more than just an interesting bit of information. It showed that if the path of storm systems is known, weather can be forecast. But weather predictions had to wait until a quicker way to send news was invented. After all, by the time stage coach mail brought the observations, the storm had already come and gone.

The invention of the telegraph by Samuel Morse made possible the rapid collection of weather information. When this was mapped, the course of severe storms could be predicted early enough to send out storm warnings. This service was so valuable that a Federal Weather Bureau was started in 1870.

At first, information gathered by the Weather Bureau was of limited use to ships at sea. Display stations were set up along the coast lines to warn passing ships with a system of flags and lights. This method is still used today, but it is of value mainly to small ships that do not have radios. It is not unusual for a radio weather report to include such information as, "Small craft warnings are being displayed from Cape Hatteras to Block Island."

The invention of the radio made it possible for ships far at sea to receive storm warnings. Also, they could send out information about weather conditions at their position on the ocean. The first weather observation from a ship at sea was sent by the S.S. *New York* in 1905. Its location at that time was 40° N. Lat. and 60° W. Long.

Today a vast network of weather-observation stations circles the earth. From Station Alert at Dumb Bell Bay on Ellesmere Island which is only 518 miles from the North Pole; from the International Geophysical Year Station at the South Pole; from U.S. Coast Guard–maintained ship stations at sea; from amateur aids in small towns, the weather news comes flooding in. After this information is mapped, the weather man is ready to make his predictions.

These predictions are sometimes of great help to you in planning a trip or a picnic, but you may be sure that the U.S. Congress does not vote to spend millions of dollars just to make your picnic a success. Weather charts are among the most important maps of the world. The safety of air travel depends on these maps. For example, weather charts were among the few maps Lindbergh used in planning his flight across the Atlantic. These showed the type of weather he could expect while crossing. They charted the prevailing winds and thus helped him decide how much gasoline he would need.

Weather maps have also helped to save thousands of lives on land. By plotting the probable course of a hurricane on a map, warnings can be given. These warnings allow time to remove people, animals, and valuables from dangerous places. The story of two hurricanes shows us the importance of storm warnings. In October, 1893, an unannounced hurricane swept into New Orleans bringing with it a great tidal wave and killing about 2,000 people. In September, 1947, the eye of a hurricane passed over New Orleans again. Although there was millions of dollars in property damage, this time, because of early warning, only twelve lives were lost.

Not all weather warning services are as dramatic as the hurricane service. Fruit farmers, for example, are also dependent on forecasts. An orange will freeze if the temperature drops to 27°, and so the fruit growers of California and Florida watch the weather maps carefully. Southern California alone has more than 3,000,000 oil burners waiting in the orchards to protect the fruit if the temperature goes down to the danger point. Summer hailstorms can also wipe out whole crops. In some parts of the country, farmers have banded together to set up a cloud-seeding service. Whenever a hailstorm warning is received, the clouds are seeded so that they will drop their moisture as rain rather than as hail.

Weather maps may even determine if you will have a day off from school. Principals and superintendents depend on weather forecasts to help them decide if the snow or sleet is bad enough to close school.

Weather forecasters use many kinds of maps. Separate maps are made to show the differences in air pressure at various altitudes. Those for the surface level and the 10,000-foot level are most common. Drawn on these maps are *isobars* (eye'so·bars) which are lines showing where the air pressure is the same.

Charts showing temperatures are also made. *Isotherms* (eye'so·therms) are drawn on these maps. An isotherm is a line running through places which have

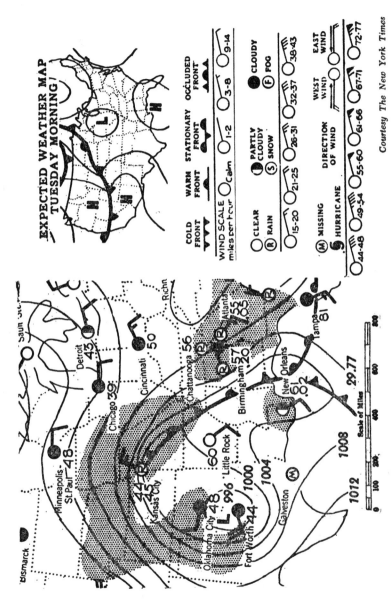

EXPECTED WEATHER MAP
TUESDAY MORNING

COLD FRONT

WARM FRONT

STATIONARY FRONT

OCCLUDED FRONT

WIND SCALE
miles per hour

Calm

1-2

3-8

9-14

15-20

21-25

26-31

32-37

38-43

44-48

49-54

55-60

61-66

67-71

72-77

CLEAR

RAIN (R)

PARTLY CLOUDY

SNOW (S)

CLOUDY

FOG (F)

MISSING (M)

HURRICANE

DIRECTION OF WIND

WEST WIND

EAST WIND

Courtesy The New York Times

the same temperature. In studying science, you will often find words beginning with "iso-." This comes from a Greek word meaning equal. Whenever you see "iso-" as part of a word, you will know that it means "the same."

Winds Aloft Charts, with arrows to show the direction of the winds, are much used by both weather forecasters and airplane navigators. These are made for such levels as 4,000 feet, 6,000 feet, 10,000 feet, 14,000 feet, etc. The weather observer sends up small balloons. From their drift, he can tell the wind direction at the higher levels. He also uses *radiosondes* (ray'dee·o·sonds) to find out more about the upper levels of the air. A radiosonde is a box of weather instruments attached to a balloon. In the box there is a thermometer to measure temperature, a barometer to measure air pressure, a hygrometer to measure moisture, and a small radio sending set. This uses a code of dots and dashes to send the information collected by the instruments back to the weather observer on the ground.

Climate maps are used to show average weather conditions. *Mean* is another word for average, and you can find charts showing monthly and yearly mean rainfall and mean temperatures. These maps are helpful not only to weather forecasters, but also to people who are planning to start a new industry or to plant a new kind of crop. No one would want to start a factory where much material had to be stored out of doors in an area with a very high average rainfall. By comparing climate charts for many years, it also is possible to see if the climate of a place is changing.

The weather charts you will see most often are the surface weather maps. These are the ones you can find in the newspapers. Surface weather maps show the position of air masses. If you were to visit the North Pole, you would expect to find very cold air. Along the equator you would expect warm air. Just as the drops of water in the ocean are constantly moving, the air too is always in motion. Great masses of cold air from the polar regions of Canada sweep down across the North American continent. Warm, moist air flows northward from the Gulf of Mexico. The advancing edge of a polar air mass is marked on the map as a *Cold Front*. A *Warm Front* is the advancing side of a tropical air mass. The weather changes when a new front moves in.

Surface weather maps are shaded to show rain and snow. There are special symbols to mark thunderstorms. Sometimes the temperatures at important weather stations are printed on the map. Some surface weather maps show areas of high and low pressure. Isobars are drawn on such maps to show where the pressure is the same.

NOW TRY THIS

Try making your own predictions by using daily weather charts taken from a newspaper. You will need to collect maps for several days so that you will have some idea how fast the air masses are moving. In making predictions you will need to remember the following weather facts:

1. Weather in the Northern Hemisphere generally moves from west to east. Normally it moves about 600 miles in twenty-four hours.

2. Cold fronts and high-pressure areas tend to move southeast.

3. Warm fronts and low-pressure areas tend to move northeast.

4. Areas of low pressure usually carry storms.

5. Areas of high pressure usually have fair weather.

6. Weather changes when a new front moves in.

It is fun to see if your predictions come true. Probably you will be right only part of the time, but even the most learned scientist 100 years ago could not predict the weather as accurately as you can.

9. Mapping the Round Earth

Through the ages, scientists and other wise men have learned many facts about the earth. Often they have shared their knowledge by picturing it on maps. Sometimes they have gained knowledge by drawing maps. But one thing they have never learned is how to make a flat map of the earth tell the whole truth. Flat maps can tell us many important facts, but no matter how hard the map maker tries, a flat map of a round world will always tell some things which are not true.

Scientists have learned the secrets of atomic energy. Aviators can fly faster than sound. You can send your voice winging over the ocean by radio telephone, but no one can flatten out a globe without tearing, stretching, or crumpling it.

A perfect flat map of the world would have four things: the shapes of the land masses and the oceans would be correct; their sizes would be accurate; it would be possible to find the exact distance between any two places on the map by using the scale; and each place on the map would be found in the right direction from every other place. Every flat map of the earth you have ever seen has been distorted in one way or another.

114

NOW TRY THIS

A baseball can help you understand some of the map makers' problems. Cut a circle out of tissue paper. If you are using a hard ball, the circle should be 9 inches in *diameter*. (The distance across the center of a circle or through the center of a sphere is its diameter.) Cover the baseball as carefully as you can with the paper. Find the sewing lines on the ball

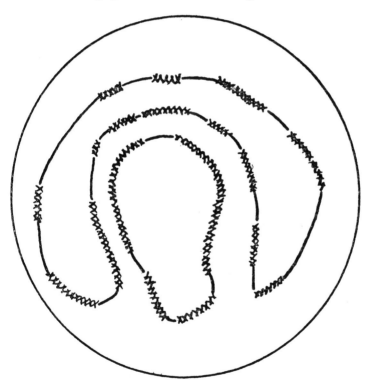

FLAT MAP OF A BASEBALL

and trace them with a pencil. Unwrap and smooth out the paper. You will find that the lines are not connected. Use a colored pencil to join the broken lines. This new line is longer and its shape is different from the original line on your baseball. This is what would happen if a map maker tried to make a flat picture of a globe in this way.

If globes are more truthful, why bother with flat maps? Imagine the chart room of a yacht about to sail from Boston for Cocos Island. It would need a globe to show prevailing winds, a globe to show ocean depths and currents, a globe to be used with radio bearings, celestial globes to show the heavens in both the Northern and Southern Hemispheres, and finally, a globe big enough to show the coast line of Cocos Island.

Since the whole island is only 15 miles long, a globe the size of the famous Langlois Globe of Paris, the scale of which is about 5 miles to 1 inch, would be needed. The distance around the equator on the Langlois Globe is 410 feet. The diameter is 128 feet. A globe this size would cover the whole deck of a ship like the *Mayflower,* and hang over 13 feet at both the prow and the stern. Of course, the overhang on each side would be much greater.

Perhaps you would rather imagine your family car ready for a trip across the state. Fastened to the roof would be a global road map about the size of the two-ton aluminum globe in the Daily News Building in New York City. This one has a scale of 55 miles to 1 inch, and the distance around its equator is only about 38 feet! The flat road maps which you can fold up and keep in the glove compartment of your car usually have a scale of from 10 to no more than 20 miles to 1 inch for a single state.

Obviously, flat maps are needed not only for convenience, but also to show the details of small areas. Flat maps of small areas can be made accurately. If you want to trace on tissue paper an inch or two of the sewing line on your baseball, you can do it easily and exactly. The earth is so tremendous that the curve at any one place is very slight. For this reason, flat maps which show only a city, a state, or a small country are accurate enough for general purposes. The real trouble arises when the map maker tries to show a continent, a hemisphere, or the entire earth on a flat map.

Of course, no map is really made by wrapping a piece of tissue around a globe as you did with the baseball. A map maker uses geometry to help him make flat maps of the round world. When you show slides or movie films on a screen, you are projecting them. When a map maker shows a round globe on a flat surface, he makes a *projection* (pro·jec'shun) of the globe. Different kinds of projections are made for different purposes.

Most maps of large areas of the earth are projected

in one of three ways: onto a cylinder; onto a cone; or onto a flat or plane surface. A flat map is made from a cylinder or cone by splitting it along a line and opening it out. A map made from one of these projections will be accurate only where the projection touches the globe, but the areas close to this point of contact also will be reasonably accurate.

A cylinder will touch the globe along the equator, so cylindrical projections are accurate for the equatorial regions. A cone touches the globe at the 40th parallel. Since this parallel passes through the United States, a conic projection of the Northern Hemisphere can be used to map the United States.

A plane projection is sometimes called a *polar projection,* but the touching point does not need to be one of the poles. *Polar cases,* which are plane projections touching one of the poles, are very common. But a map can be made which touches the globe at any place: for example, your home town. Again, the map

PROJECTIONS

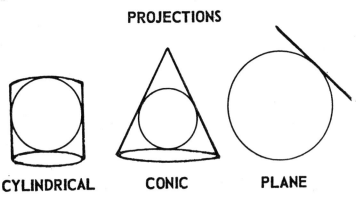

CYLINDRICAL   CONIC   PLANE

is accurate for the touching point and reasonably accurate for a circle around it.

In the following diagrams a picture of a dog has been projected by these four different methods. As you can see, each of these projections has its faults.

Map makers have tried to correct these distortions by changing the projections to suit their needs. Gerardus Mercator, a Dutch map maker who lived in the 1500s, made the best-known variation of the cylindri-

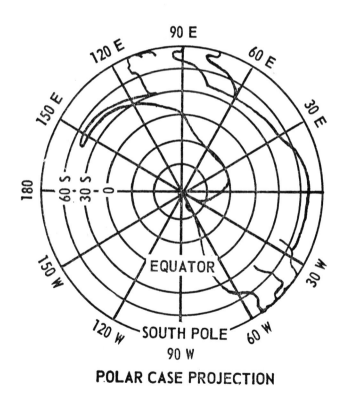

POLAR CASE PROJECTION

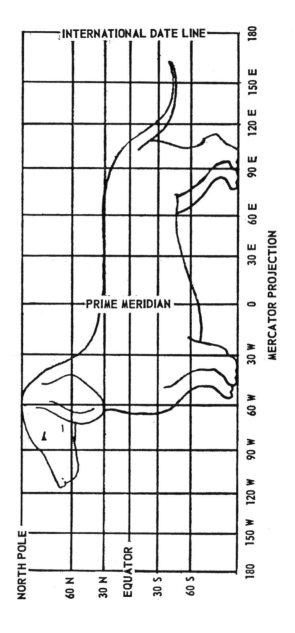

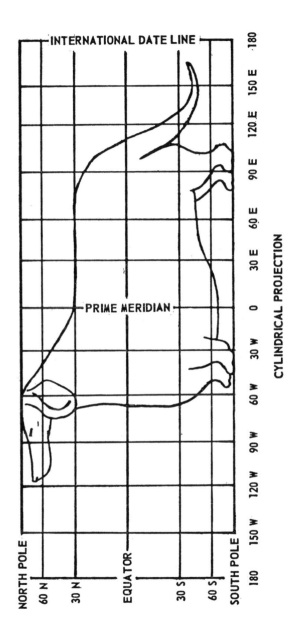

CYLINDRICAL PROJECTION

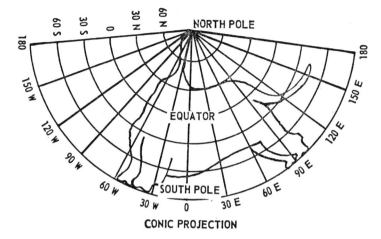

CONIC PROJECTION

cal projection.   The Mercator projection is most important to navigators.

As long as ships stayed close to the shores of Europe, the curve of the earth did not matter much to the chart makers.   *Portolan charts* which were made and used by the sailors of the Middle Ages are an example. These maps are covered with straight lines which follow the directions marked on the compass rose.   A line which follows one direction all the way is called a *rhumb line*.   On a map of a small area, a rhumb line appears to be straight.   It is always straight on a Mercator projection, but on all other projections of the globe, a long rhumb line is a curve.

The rhumb line course of a ship sailing North East by North from the mouth of the Amazon River on the equator (0° Lat. and 50° W. Long.) to Land's End, England (49°50′ N. Lat. and 6°27′ W. Long.) is

plotted on each of the four projections in the illustration. You can see that it is a straight line only on the
Mercator projection.

The easiest course for a sailor to follow is a rhumb
line. His compass direction will be the same for the
entire voyage, but he must allow for drift caused by
winds and sea currents. Land's End is due North
East by North from the mouth of the Amazon River
and there are no islands or other obstacles in the way.
Therefore, it might seem that a rhumb line course
would be the shortest distance between the two, but

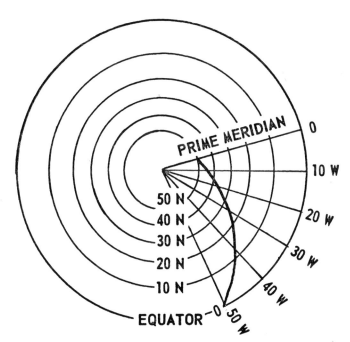

NE by N RHUMB LINE ON POLAR CASE PROJECTION

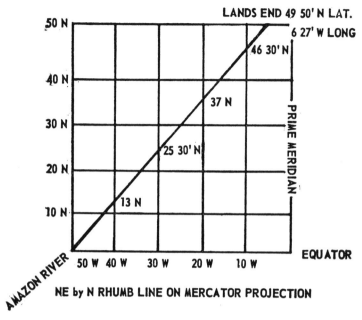

NE by N RHUMB LINE ON MERCATOR PROJECTION

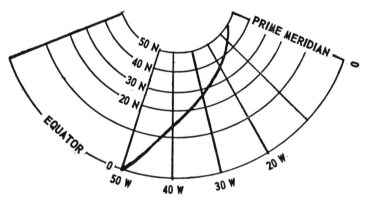

NE by N RHUMB LINE ON CONIC PROJECTION

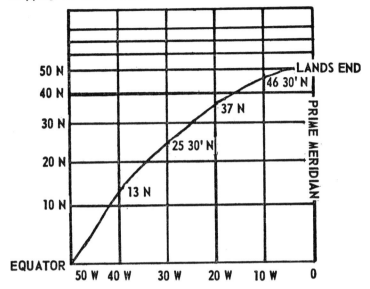

NE by N RHUMB LINE ON CYLINDRICAL PROJECTION

this is not true. If the earth were flat, a rhumb line would be the shortest distance between two points. But the curve of the earth, which makes so much trouble for the map maker, also plays tricks on the navigator. It is about 275 miles farther from the Amazon to Land's End by rhumb line than by a *great circle* route.

It is possible to draw many circles on the face of a globe. Some of the circles go completely around the earth and divide it into two equal parts. These are called great circles. There are also *lesser circles,* such as the parallels of latitude (except the equator) which do not divide the globe into equal parts. (See page 55.) The equator and the meridian circles are good examples of great circles, but a great circle can be drawn so that it passes through any two places on the globe. The shortest route between these two places will follow this great circle.

Making the map in sections is still another way of projecting the round earth onto a flat surface. Most globes are made of sections which are printed on flat pieces of paper and then stretched and glued to a sphere.

Sometimes map makers "peel" the globe and make maps which have curious shapes. These are called *interrupted maps* because they show blank spaces between the parts of the maps.

Looking at a globe is like viewing the earth from Mars. As you go farther away from a thing, it looks smaller and you can see fewer details. An airplane may appear as a dot in the sky and still be larger than a house, as you can see when you stand beside it. If you were on Mars, the earth would appear to be a smooth, shiny ball like a globe. Of course, you only need to look out the window to know that this is not true. The surface of the earth is rippled with bumps and dents, hills and valleys, mountains and ocean deeps.

Relief maps which show the uneven surface or *contour* of the earth are needed by such people as engineers, travelers, and airplane pilots. The people of

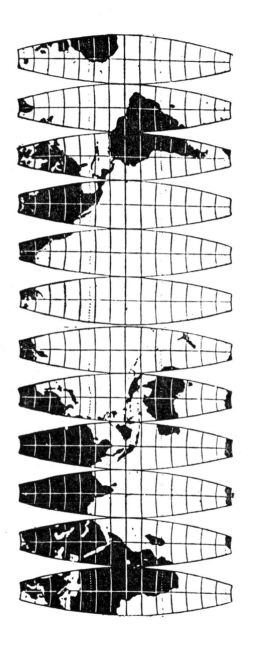

12 GORE MAP

ancient China drew little hills on their maps to show the location of mountains. You can see this method used today on maps in newspapers and magazines. Everyone knows what is meant by a little row of hills on a map, but you cannot tell the height of the mountains or the area which they cover.

Relief maps can be made by building up the contours of the land on a flat surface. Perhaps you, yourself, have made a map of this kind out of clay or plaster of Paris. These *three-dimensional maps* are useful because they help you see the shape of the land very clearly. Except for maps of small areas, however, they must be distorted. The earth is so large that, unless the scale is distorted, even Mt. Everest would be smaller than a pin head on a map of the world one yard square. The largest three-dimensional map of the United States is in the Babson Institute in Wellesley Hills, Massachusetts. It is made on a curved surface and has a scale of about 4 miles to 1 inch. To make the contours stand out, the distorted scale for height is six times greater.

Plastic three-dimensional maps which are made by some companies are light and convenient to store. But most three-dimensional maps are expensive and clumsy to handle, so another way of showing contours is needed. Long ago, artists discovered that they could draw pictures without outlines. They used a system of lines to show lights and shadows.

Using lines in this way to show contours is called

hachuring (ha·shur'ing). The hachuring lines on a map are drawn in the direction water flows across the surface of the land. Many of the hachured maps made during the 1800s were works of art. Because they required such great skill, a simpler form, the *caterpillar map* was devised.

Most map makers today use *contour lines* to show the surface of the earth. Just as isobars on weather maps (see page 110) connect areas of equal pressure, contour lines connect areas of equal height. Sometimes the height is printed along the lines. Many maps use different colors to show different heights. These are especially useful for airplane pilots who need to know mountain heights quickly.

Because maps of small areas are less distorted and

HACHURE MAP   **CATERPILLAR MAP**

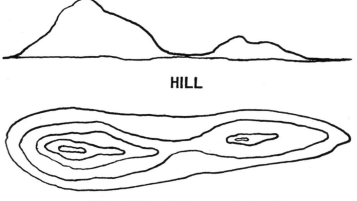

HILL

CONTOUR LINES OF THE HILL

show more details than maps of large areas, many map makers prefer to chart the earth in small sections and then group them in an *atlas*. In the legends of the ancient Greeks, Atlas is the giant who carries the entire world on his shoulders. When Mercator published an atlas of maps bound in one book, he included a family tree showing the ancestors of Atlas. His "atlas" was so popular that soon any collection of maps bound in one book came to be called an atlas. But Mercator was not the first map maker to make such a collection.

The first known atlas was prepared by Claudius Ptolemy of Alexandria, who lived from 90 A.D. to 168 A.D. It was part of a set of books called *Geographia*. The finest medieval atlas is the *Catalan Atlas* which can be seen in the Bibliothèque Nationale (National Library) in Paris. It contains Portolan charts of Europe and maps of Asia made from Marco Polo's descriptions of his travels. The many modern atlases which are published today are the dictionaries and encyclopedias of the map-making world.

The story of maps in this book has been told in terms of the needs of the traveler: the airplane pilot, the sailor, and your father in his car. Many of the biggest and most exciting advances in map making were developed to help travelers. But it is important to remember that maps are also very useful to those who stay at home.

10. Mapping the Make-believe, the Almost Real, and the Real

Some maps belong to the just-for-fun group. Run your finger down the map of the coast line of North America and then trace the shapes of the islands of the Caribbean. You have just touched the hiding places of billions of dollars of treasure. Somewhere along these coasts lie the loot of pirates and the water-logged treasures of wrecked ships. Key West, Catalina Island, Gardiners Island, Plum Point, and Oak Island—all these are magic names to the seekers of lost treasure.

The search for hidden treasure has attracted men from earliest times. Rich man, poor man, beggar man, thief; everyone loves to dream of finding buried treasure. In July, 1934, the President of the United States, traveling from Puerto Rico to Hawaii, went ashore on a tiny island off the west coast of Panama. Why should a man as busy as President Roosevelt take time to visit an island inhabited only by goats? He did it because it is a very special island, Cocos, the burial place of three great treasures.

Legend tells us that the first treasure was left there by the English pirate, Edgar Davis, who banked his loot on those lonely shores. Then, during a revolution in Peru in 1812, the treasures of the cathedral of Lima

COOS BAY, ORE.

OAK IS.

BOOTHBAY HARBOR ME.

POINT ARGUELLO CAL.

CRESCENT CITY, CAL.

SNAKE IS. (John Quelch)

(Cap. Kidd)

NEW YORK HARBOR

GARDINERS ISLAND (Capt. Kidd)

SANTA CATALINA ISLAND

SAN LUIS REY, CAL. (Cortes)

LEWES, DEL.

SANTA BARBARA, CAL.

PLUM POINT, N.C. (Blackbeard)

VERO BEACH FLA.

SABINE (La Fitte)

BOCA RATON FLA.

PADRES IS. TEX. (La Fitte)

BAHAMA IS.

GRASSY KEY

PORT ROYAL

CHAGRES RIVER PANAMA (Morgan)

ISLA DES CANOS (Drake)

COCOS IS. (3 Treasures)

MAP OF A FEW OF THE MANY LEGENDARY TREASURES

were said to have been given into the care of Captain Thompson of the ship *Mary Dyer*. But things were so bad in Peru that he decided to bury them on the north end of Cocos Island until he could return them to the rightful owners. Seven years later, the Mexican bandit, Benito Bonito, chose the same island to hide millions of dollars of silver which he had stolen from the Mexican treasure trains. These three stories have attracted many parties of treasure hunters, including the President of the United States. But so far, only one silver crucifix has been found, and the goats of Cocos Island are still the richest goats in the world.

Since Cocos Island is so very small, less than 15 square miles, why has no one discovered any treasure? If you were to visit this rocky island with its waterfalls, caves, and sandy beaches, you would see that it is impossible to dig up the entire place. To find treasure, you would need a map showing where it is located. No real treasure maps of Cocos Island are known to exist, but perhaps somewhere there may be a well-worn chart waiting to be found. Certainly, many false treasure maps of Cocos have come to light. After the silver crucifix was discovered in 1903, false maps were made and sold in England. These map makers had found a way to collect treasure without ever setting foot on Cocos Island.

Cocos Island is not the only place that has attracted false map makers. Maps claiming to show the hiding places of the treasures of Captain Kidd, Blackbeard, Henry Morgan, and others appear all the time. Perhaps no real pirate maps do exist, but we do know that the pirates who sailed the seas so many years ago were unable to keep their riches in banks. So, we think that they may have buried their loot on uninhabited islands. It is easy to see how the legends of pirate maps grew. Certainly, if such maps ever existed, they must have been very poor. With only a compass to help him, the pirate would have had to depend mainly on unreliable landmarks.

You will probably never find a real treasure map, but there are plenty of imaginary ones waiting for you between the covers of books. A good example of such a map can be found in Robert Louis Stevenson's book *Treasure Island.* It is believed that Stevenson based his map on a real map of Cocos Island. Look at the two maps on the next pages. You can see that they are somewhat similar.

Everyone knows that such maps as the one in *Treasure Island* are make-believe. But there are real maps of imaginary places. The makers of these maps honestly believed that the lands which they drew existed. During the fifteenth and sixteenth centuries, when the countries of Europe first started to explore the rest of the world, maps were state secrets, guarded as carefully as today's atom bomb secrets. In most countries, it was an act of treason, punishable by death, to sell or give a navigation chart to a foreign nation.

There were two reasons for this. First, since each European country wanted to claim as much new land as possible, you can be sure no country wanted to help its neighbor by sharing its maps. Second, maps were difficult to make, for each one had to be drawn carefully by hand. A map maker would work a long,

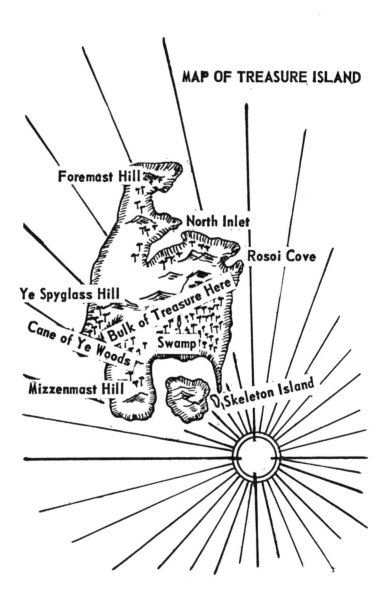

MAP OF TREASURE ISLAND

Foremast Hill

North Inlet

Rosoi Cove

Ye Spyglass Hill

Bulk of Treasure Here

Cane of Ye Woods

Swamp

Mizzenmast Hill

D, Skeleton Island

long time to prepare charts from the information brought back from one expedition. Some of the travelers who brought back information for the map makers had very good imaginations and so you will find "Isles of Satan," "Isles of Goats," and many other strange islands dotting the North Atlantic Ocean.

One such legendary island was named Buss. It was "sighted" first about 1578, somewhat south of Greenland. It was reported to be one of the largest islands on earth and many expeditions set out to explore it. Although they searched carefully, the nearest thing to an island that ever appeared was an upturned boat bottom covered with moss. But the map makers hated to give up the island and so Buss appears on maps made as late as 1745. By that time, however, it was reduced to a "surf" ¼ mile long surrounded by a rough sea.

The most famous lost island is Atlantis. The story of this tremendous continent in the middle of the Atlantic originated about 2,300 years ago. It is described as being unbelievably wealthy, with cities and streets of gold. Old maps sometimes show Atlantis located in the Sargasso Sea. Although it supposedly disappeared into the ocean many centuries ago, Atlantis is still a favorite location for the writers of imaginative books and movies.

Of course, there are real maps of real treasure. These are the maps which show where oil, gold, or uranium may be found. If it is impossible to find the treasures of Cocos Island by digging up a mere 15 square miles, imagine how hard it would be to find the treasures of the earth if prospectors had to dig up the entire 9 million square miles of North America. Again, maps are needed to pin-point the treasure. But the modern maps differ from the older ones. There is no "*X*" to mark the spot where the treasure is hidden. Instead, these maps show the kinds of rock that probably lie under the surface of the earth. With this information, a *geologist* (gee·ol'oh·jist), a scientist who studies rock formations, can guess where such modern treasures as oil, natural gas, or uranium may be found.

Modern treasure maps may be prepared by private

companies. In this case, they are guarded almost as carefully as were the maps of fifteenth century Europe. The U.S. Government, through its Geological Survey, also prepares such maps. A map which shows the rock formation of the land is called a *geologic map.* Geologic maps of many sections of the United States may be bought from the Geological Survey in Washington, D.C. One such geologic map shows a rock formation in New York State in which oil might be found.

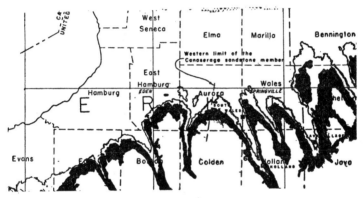

The industries hunting for modern treasures are not the only businesses which have special maps made for their own use. Transportation industries need maps all the time. Trucking companies, for example, use maps that show the weight which bridges will support and the height of underpasses. It is most important to them not to route a 10-ton truck over a bridge which is strong enough to hold only 2 tons. Nor can they send a 15-foot truck through a 12-foot underpass. Other businesses also use maps. These may show where each branch is located, or where each salesman is working, or where raw materials are available.

Industries are not the only users of maps which are not made just for travelers. There are "stay-at-home" maps which are of great importance to you and your family. The oldest and perhaps the most valuable of these are the *land use maps*. These are maps of small areas which show the division, ownership, and use of the land. The oldest existing land use maps were made on clay tablets in Babylon over 4,000 years ago. The newest ones are still on the drawing boards of the map makers. There is a map showing the lot on which your house is built on file in your County Courthouse.

Another type of land use map has become important recently. For many years, cities just grew. People put up houses and made streets wherever they wanted. One famous exception to this is Washington, D.C. It was planned by the French architect, Pierre l'Enfant, who used a system of circles and spokes spreading out from the Capitol. But beyond the area of his original map, even Washington has grown without a plan. Today we know it is important to make plans of our cities to show: here we will have homes; over here will be the shops; and there we can build factories. This is called zoning, and most cities and towns today have *zoning maps*.

Both the state and federal governments issue many

different kinds of maps. There are maps which show the voting districts of an area so that each citizen will know where to vote. There are maps of the forest preserves; the Army and the Navy have many, many maps; there are maps showing the density of population across our country. In fact, there is no department in our government which does not use maps.

You may wonder why they make all these special types of maps. They could write out the information instead of plotting it on a map. But imagine, if you can, how many pages of writing it would take to describe the boundaries of every lot in even a very small village! And yet, it can all be shown very clearly on a single map. There is a famous saying, "One picture is worth a thousand words." And a map is a very useful picture.

Index